Soap Making for Beginners

100 Simple and Easy-to-Follow Soap Recipes

Table of Contents

Introduction

Have you actually ever used soap before?

Most people have never used soap in their entire lives.

And I don't refer to third-world countries, poor people, or just people who refuse to use soaps and maintain their "natural odor"...I speak about normal people who shower every day, wash their hands, and condition their hair. Yes, that's right – that includes you.

Commercial soap sold in retail stores is mostly made from artificial chemicals, hardeners and synthetic lathering materials. Some of these ingredients are actually *dangerous* to your skin.

On the other hand, soaps that are made by the hand like they used to be made for centuries, are very beneficial to the skin and to your health and looks. Handmade soap is made from natural oils and liquids and does not contain harsh chemicals.

This book contains all the essential information about soap making:

- What you need to get started

- A step-by-step guide for different soap-making processes

- And 100 simple soap recipes that every newbie can make.

The soap recipes in this book follow either the melt-and-pour method—for those who are not ready to deal with lye yet—or the cold process technique. Both are great for beginners and the instructions are explained in detail so you won't have to make any guesses or go back to the guide every time you make soap.

The recipes are grouped into three categories. In the first group, you will find recipes which require only four or five ingredients. Any one of them will be the perfect choice for your first ever handmade soap.

The second group is for beauty soaps, with each recipe indicating what it's best used for. They vary from simple four-ingredient melt-and-pour recipes to more complicated cold process soap recipes.

The last group of recipes is for making beautiful soaps with several colors, layers, or swirl patterns. Although these recipes are a bit challenging and take some practice to create, they're perfect for when you're ready to step up your soap-making game.

Lastly, you will learn how to use a lye calculator. While this isn't essential for beginners, knowing this may come in handy if you need to make small changes in the soap recipe.

Chapter 1
Soap Making 101

Soap making is an age-old tradition, which has almost vanished due to the availability of commercial soaps. While people from yesteryears didn't have a choice but to make their own soap, more people these days are opting for handmade soaps as a natural alternative to chemical-rich, store-bought soaps.

But how is soap exactly made?

What most people don't know about soap is that it's actually salt. If you still remember your high school chemistry, you'll know that salt is a product of the chemical reaction between an acid and a base. Indeed, soap is made from an animal- or plant-derived fats and oils (which are acids) and lye (which is a base).

When these two are combined, a chemical reaction known as saponification takes place. But soap isn't the only product of this reaction. During saponification, glycerin—a chemical compound that moisturizes the skin—is formed as a natural byproduct.

Lye is a dangerous chemical because of its high alkalinity. One drop can burn the skin or cause permanent eye damage if not rinsed properly. It's the potential danger of lye and the seemingly intimidating process that keep many people from soap making.

Fortunately for you, you can now make your own handmade soap with or without lye. The methods that involve lye and those that don't are entirely different. But whichever method you choose, you'll find that soap making is fun and fulfilling.

Choosing Essential Equipment and Ingredients

Before you can start making soap, you need to have the necessary materials. You don't need high-end apparatus but you need to gather equipment and ingredients that are suitable for soap making. Below is a list of the must-haves and what to consider when purchasing them.

Soap Making Equipment

1. Digital Scale

In soap making, all the oils, butters, water, and lye must be measured by weight and not by volume. This is because measuring cups from different manufacturers can vary in size. There's also the tendency of anyone who uses these cups to fill them with less or more. Although the difference may be small, you could end up with a soap that's too oily or lye-heavy, which is unsafe.

You don't need a fancy scale when making soap. You can get one from any store selling kitchen supplies.

2. Containers

You need several containers:

- *For measuring lye*

  Use small disposable cups or a small container marked with the word **lye**.

- *For mixing lye*

  When you add to water, the solution can heat up to 200°F so it's important to use a heat-proof container. A heavy-duty plastic container with a recycle #5 symbol or a stainless steel container is best. Avoid using glass since reaction with lye can cause weak points and accidental breakage.

- *For measuring/holding liquid oil*

You can use any type of container since this will only hold the liquid oils before you add them to the melted solid oils.

- *For melting oils/soap base and mixing soap*

  Depending on how you will melt the oils, you can use a microwave-safe bowl, Pyrex mixing pitcher, or a large pot. This container should be big enough to mix all the ingredients and deep enough so you can mix the batter without splashing it around.

- *For mixing different color*

  Some recipes may require you to divide the soap batter so you can color them separately. You can use any container except for aluminum or anything with Teflon since they react negatively to the soap batter.

3. Thermometer

When working with lye, you'll have to add or mix ingredients within a certain temperature range. To do this, you should have a reliable and accurate thermometer.

You can use a candy thermometer if that's what you already have. But for ease of use and convenience, it's best to invest in an infrared thermometer. This tool can tell you the temperature in less than a second with high accuracy. And because it doesn't use a probe, there's no need to clean it after each use.

4. Stick Blender (Immersion Blender)

Soap making involves a lot of mixing and stirring. Even though you can definitely mix soap by hand, it's time-consuming and could take hours depending on the ingredients and how much soap you're making. With a stick or immersion blender, you can cut that time to just a few minutes.

When you're just starting, it's fine to use an inexpensive stick blender. But if you intend to make soap regularly, it's wise to have a durable blender.

5. Spoons and Spatulas

You will use these for preparing the lye solution, stirring the oils and soap batter, and scraping bits of soap left in the mixing pot. Choose spoons or spatulas made with silicone or heavy-duty plastic, and go for those with long handles. Avoid anything with aluminum.

6. Safety Gears

Gloves and goggles are an absolute must when you're working with lye. This chemical is caustic and can leave burn marks on your skin.

Use dishwashing or disposable nitrile or latex gloves to protect your hands. To protect your eyes, use safety goggles specifically made for handling chemicals.

7. Soap Molds

There are so many types and shapes of molds you can use when making soap. They range from pricey wooden molds to free repurposed containers and boxes.

- *Silicone Molds*

  Molds made with silicone are the best because they're ready to use as is and they come in different shapes and sizes. They're quite flexible so they make the removal of soap a breeze. If you're using a mold with individual cavities, there's no need to cut the soap.

  When using silicone molds, you have to insulate them well if you want your cold-process soap to fully gel.

- *Wooden loaf and slab molds*

  Soap in wooden mold normally doesn't require added insulation to gel, unless it's cold. If you're going to use this type of mold, you have to line it with wax paper or freezer paper. It's also best to choose a mold that's made with untreated hardwood since unsaponified soap can react to treated wood.

- *PVC pipes*

  These are great for making round soap. You don't have to line them but smearing some mineral oil will help make the removal of soap much easier.

- *Plastic or cardboard food* containers

  Yogurt cups, milk cartons, and cream cheese containers can be used as molds. These are great if you're just starting out, you're working with small batches, or there's leftover soap after you've poured into your prepared mold. They don't have to be lined and once soap hardens, you can simply peel the container away.

- *Tupperware containers/plastic boxes*

  You don't need to line these molds unless they're thick and not that flexible. Soap should be insulated well to achieve a full gel.

- *Cardboard boxes*

  Cardboard boxes, such as sturdy shoe boxes, need to be lined when used as molds. Proper insulation is also necessary for this one.

8. Cutting Board and Knife/Soap Cutter

If you're making melt-and-pour soap, you'll have to cut the soap base, which comes in large blocks, so they'll melt faster. And if you put your soap in a large mold, you'll have to cut it when it becomes firm.

9. Other supplies

- Spray bottle of alcohol – to remove bubbles and make layers of soap stick together, if you're making melt-and-pour soap; to reduce the formation of soda ash

- Paper towels and white vinegar – to wipe away and neutralize spills of lye or splashes of raw soap

- Small bowls – for measuring and holding essential oil, fragrance oil, colorants, and other additives

- Wax paper – for lining or covering molds

- Cardboard and towel/blanket – to cover and insulate the soap

Soap Making Ingredients

Oils, Fats, and Butters

Most soap recipes contain 3 to 6 oils and kinds of butter. Different oils contribute to different properties and knowing these will give you an idea what to expect with your soap in terms of hardness, conditioning, lather, and creaminess.

Apricot kernel oil is high in vitamins A, C, and E. It's highly conditioning, moisturizing, and absorbs easily. It produces a stable creamy lather with small bubbles. This oil is lightweight and using too much (more than 15%) will make soap bars that are too soft and won't last long in the shower.

Argan oil makes soap feel silky. It's highly moisturizing, as well as rich in antioxidants and vitamins A and E.

Avocado butter has a creamy consistency. It moisturizes the skin and makes it feel smooth.

Avocado oil is high in amino acids, beta-carotene, potassium, protein, and vitamins A, B, D, and E. It helps in healing sun-damaged skin and is good for mature or aging skin. Avocado oil in soaps makes it soft so your soap should only have up to 20% of it.

Babassu oil comes from a certain type of palm tree. It's high in antioxidants and vitamin E, and good for both oily and dry skin. Because of its cleansing and firming properties, it can replace palm or coconut oil in a cold-process soap recipe.

Beeswax will add a bit of hardness to your soap and is a great addition to shampoo bars. It's only used in small amounts in soap making since it reduces lather. It also speeds up trace so if it's your first time making cold-process soap, avoid those recipes that include beeswax.

Black cumin seed oil or black seed oil has anti-oxidants and anti-inflammatory properties. It's known as a natural skincare and haircare aid. It can be used to make a gentle cleanser that soothes irritated skin.

Canola oil gives the soap a dense creamy lather. It's inexpensive and can be used as an alternative for olive oil.

Castor oil is a thick liquid derived from the castor bean plant. It is easily absorbed into the skin and creates a soap with amazing lather. It's great for making shampoo bars, too. Ideally, your soap shouldn't have more than 10% of castor oil since too much can make it soft and sticky.

Cocoa butter makes soap extra moisturizing and feels luxurious. It should only be used in small amounts since too much may cause soap to crack or easily melt.

Coconut oil is one of the most common oils used in soap making and it's known for its excellent cleansing power. However, it strips oils off the skin as it cleanses so if you're making soap for dry or sensitive skin, make sure that it doesn't have more than 15% of coconut oil.

Flaxseed oil contains essential fatty acids in the right proportion that gives it special healing and skin-renewing properties. You can use up to 5% of this oil in cold-process soap.

Grapeseed oil is lightweight, thin, and high in antioxidants. It's non-comedogenic, making it great for oily or acne-prone skin. Soaps with this oil can make your skin feel silky smooth.

Hazelnut oil moisturizes while cleansing the skin and is suitable for all skin types.

Hemp seed oil contains many nutrients and is rich in fatty acids. It helps keep skin hydrated and is great for dry or aging skin. Soaps with hemp seed oil make excellent lather but they also have a relatively shorter shelf life.

Jojoba oil is more like liquid wax. It contributes to a long-lasting bar of soap. It should only be used in small amounts since too much may weigh down the lather and cause pores to clog.

Lard is fat derived from pork. Recipes using lard are great for beginners since it's cheap. It also makes a long-lasting bar with a creamy lather. Freshly made soap with lard can smell like bacon but this goes away after curing.

Mango butter is high in antioxidants and vitamins A and E. It's semi-solid, melting once it touches the skin. It contributes to the soap's hardness and creates a stable, conditioning lather. Mango butter is good for dry and aging skin.

Olive oil is a thick oil that is known for its excellent moisturizing power. It's high in antioxidants but has little cleansing property. Olive oil is mild enough to be used for sensitive skin. It's great for all skin types, including a baby's skin. Pure olive oil makes a soft soap so it's best combined with hard oils or fat. Never use extra-virgin olive oil in soap making.

Palm kernel oil produces a hard cleansing bar with long-lasting lather. It can speed up trace, so only work with recipes using palm kernel oil when you're already confident with your soap-making skills. It's possible to replace this oil in a recipe with babassu or coconut oil.

Palm oil produces a hard, long-lasting bar of soap with creamy lather when combined with coconut oil. This oil is controversial since the growth of its source plant contributes to the destruction of rainforests. If you want to use this oil, choose to buy RSPO-certified palm oil.

Rice bran oil is rich in antioxidants and vitamin E. Like olive oil, it's so mild that you can make soap with 100% rice bran oil and it will still be suitable for sensitive skin.

Safflower oil is similar to canola oil. It's inexpensive, mild, and makes a softer bar of soap.

Shea butter makes soap feel silky and extra-moisturizing, just like cocoa butter. It contributes to the soap's hardness while providing a creamy lather.

Sunflower oil is rich in essential fatty acids and vitamin E and yet, it's quite inexpensive. It's possible to make soap with 100% sunflower oil but it will be soft and require more time to cure.

Sweet almond oil is a light oil that's suitable for all types of skin. It makes a soft bar of soap with a creamy lather.

Tallow, like lard, is from animal fat. It makes a hard bar of soap that's mild for the skin. It has little cleansing power, so it's usually paired with other oils.

Tamanu oil is a dark-colored oil with a nutty odor. It's moisturizing, rich in essential fatty acids, and easily absorbed into the skin.

Lye and Water

Lye is essential in soap making since soap is the product of the chemical reaction between oils and lye. Water dissolves and activates the lye and disperses it through the oils. When making soap, it's best to use distilled water.

Two types of lye are used in soap making: sodium hydroxide (NaOH) and potassium hydroxide (KOH). The latter is only used when making liquid soap.

If you want to make soap but are feeling uncomfortable about handling lye, you can still make soap following the melt-and-pour method.

Working with Lye

Lye is a strong chemical that can burn your skin if you come into contact with it. While it's dangerous, it shouldn't hold you back from making soap. By following these precautions, you'll be able to safely handle lye:

1. Before you start, remove all food from your work area and don't allow your kids or pets to get anywhere near it. Make sure that you always have quick access to running water and keep walkways clear.

2. Always wear your gloves and goggles when handling lye—even after mixing it with the oils. Avoid wearing short pants, short-sleeved shirts, or sandals.

3. Make sure that you're in a well-ventilated area when adding lye to water. Lye creates caustic steam, which you should avoid inhaling, as it dissolves in water. You can wear a face mask or wrap a bandana over your face for added protection.

4. Use distilled and chilled water. Always add lye to water. Never the other way around.

5. If your clothes get contaminated with lye, remove them immediately.

6. Always clean up spills and splashes right away.

Melt-and-Pour Soap Base

Soap bases are premade plain soaps that replace the oils, water, and lye in melt-and-pour recipes. They're usually named after the type of oil used to make it or a distinguishing ingredient.

Here are some of the most common soap bases:

- White soap base – best for making soap with a simple look; adding color results to a pastel hue

- Clear soap base – best for making vibrantly colored soap or soap with embeds or layers

- Moisturizing soap base – made of a blend of oils that cleans and moisturizes the skin; includes shea butter soap base, goat's milk soap base, olive oil soap base, honey soap base, and hemp oil soap base

Soap Fragrance

Some soap makers prefer to keep their soap unscented, leaving it to smell like a clean, handmade soap or allowing the natural aroma of oils with unique fragrance to define the scent. After all, unscented soap is best for those with exceptionally sensitive skin. If you want to give your soap a particular scent, the most common way is to add cosmetic-grade fragrance oils or essential oils.

Essential Oil Vs Fragrance Oil

Essential oils are oils derived from different parts of a plant while fragrance oils are a mix of natural and synthetic chemical components formulated to mimic the smell of something natural or to have an entirely new smell.

Essential oils are 100% natural and aside from the scent, they often carry the health benefits of the plant they were extracted from. You can't expect a fragrance oil with the same scent as an essential oil to provide you with its aromatherapy benefits.

However, it requires hundreds of pounds of plant material to produce a pound of essential oil. This makes essential oils cost a lot. And if you're new to soap making, you may want to save that money for later, when you're already sure about what you're doing.

Fragrance oils offer a more affordable way to add scent to your soap. In fact, many of them are ridiculously cheap. They're also easier to find and you have more options to choose from.

Adding Fragrance

Before using any fragrance or essential oil, make sure that you read the description and instructions first. Even though essential oils are natural, they're still chemicals and you should always take caution when putting them in something that you will use on your body.

The amount of essential or fragrance oil you can add to your soap depends on the standard usage rate for that particular oil. Many experienced soap makers usually follow a *personal* maximum oil usage rate guideline based on the standards of regulatory bodies. Coming up with this guideline takes some research, calculation, and actual soap-making experience.

The recipes in this e-book follow a stricter guideline. You can add up to 0.48 ounces of essential oil for every pound of cold-process soap. For every pound of melt-and-pour soap, you can add up to 0.25 ounces of essential oil or 0.4 ounces of fragrance oil. If you want to use more oils for a stronger scent, make sure that you do your research first on that particular oil to ensure safety.

Colorants

Some of the oils used in making soap will impart a light yellow or creamy color. But if you want your soap to have a more vibrant color, you have several options to choose from. These range from store-bought pigments to plants that you might have in your garden.

Pigments are colorants in a powdered form available in two types—oxides and ultramarines. Even though they're synthetic, they're usually made with natural materials. Their colors also mimic those of naturally occurring things, like *iron oxide red*, commonly known as rust.

When coloring with pigments, premix the colorants with oil or liquid glycerin before adding to the soap batter. A teaspoon of pigment will give a pound of base oil a dark shade of color.

Mica colorants are powdered mica—a rock-forming mineral that can be peeled off in sheets—which are sterilized and combined with dyes or pigments to give them color. When used in clear soap, they give not just color but also a sparkly appearance.

Like pigments, it's best to premix mica with liquid to avoid clumps before adding to your soap. A teaspoon of mica colorant will give a pound of base oil a bold, dark shade.

F, D, and C dyes can be bought in powdered or liquid form. A liquid dye is added directly to the soap base. The dye in powdered form has to be mixed with a little water before adding to the soap.

Clays are usually used to make soap that detoxifies and lightly exfoliates the skin, but they also give the soap a natural color.

Herbs, flowers, and roots can be used to give your soap a natural color. Commonly used plant colorants are calendula petals (golden orange), madder root (pink), and alkanet root (purple).

Botanicals

Botanicals refer to flower, leaves, fruits, and roots that you can add to your soap to impart a natural color, make it more visually appealing, or provide exfoliation.

- Dried fruits (lemon and orange slices) and spices (cinnamon sticks and apple spice) can give your soap scent- or holiday-themed designs.

- Ground almonds, poppy seeds, and walnut shell powder are some of the additives you can use to create a scrubby soap.

- Dried herbs and flowers can be used on top or in the interiors of your soap.

- Ground turmeric, madder, and alkanet roots, when added directly to your soap, can give it a natural color.

Chapter 2: Simple Soap Recipes

Melt-and-Pour Soap Recipes

Apple Pie Soap

This soap smells delicious and makes for a great holiday gift.

Ingredients

- 1 lb. shea melt-and-pour soap base
- 0.25 oz. (½ tbsp.) vanilla extract
- 0.16 oz. (1 tsp.) Apple fragrance oil
- ½ tsp. cinnamon
- red liquid colorant

Instructions

1. Cut the soap base into small cubes and place them in a microwave-safe bowl. Microwave in 30-second increments, stirring after each burst.

2. Once soap base has completely melted, add 1 to 2 drops of colorant and mix until you're satisfied with the color. Add the vanilla extract, cinnamon, and fragrance oil. Mix thoroughly.

3. Pour soap into the cavities of your mold. Spritz some alcohol on the surface if there are bubbles on your soap.

4. Allow the soap to cool and completely harden for at least 2 hours before removing from the mold.

Black Raspberry Soap

This melt-and-pour exfoliating soap is perfect for beginners. It only requires 4 ingredients and you could substitute the raspberry seeds with any exfoliant you already have, like poppy seeds. You could also swap out the madder root with any natural colorant, like paprika and turmeric.

Ingredients

- 1 lb. olive oil melt-and-pour soap base

- 0.16 oz. (1 tsp.) black raspberry scented oil

- ½ tsp. raspberry seeds

- ½ tsp. madder root powder

Instructions

1. Cut the soap base into small pieces using a kitchen knife. Place them in a microwave-safe container. Melt the soap in the microwave at 30-second intervals, stirring after each increment. Microwave until soap is fully melted.

2. Stir in the raspberry oil, raspberry seeds, and madder root. Mix until color is fully incorporated.

3. Pour soap mixture into the mold. Set aside for 2 hours or until soap is firm.

4. When the soap has completely hardened and cooled, remove it from the mold.

Cinnamon Soap

If you want to make an excellent handmade gift for men, try this recipe.

Ingredients

- 1 lb. clear melt-and-pour soap base

- 0.08 oz. (½ tsp.) cinnamon essential oil

- 1 tbsp. poppy seeds

- red liquid colorant

Instructions

1. Cut the soap base into small cubes and place them in a microwave-safe bowl. Melt the soap in the microwave at 30-second intervals, stirring in between bursts.

2. Once the soap base has completely melted, stir in the essential oil. Add the poppy seeds and a drop or two of colorant. Mix until color is fully dispersed. Feel free to add more colorant until you're satisfied with the color.

3. Pour the soap mixture into your prepared mold. Lightly spray with alcohol to get rid of bubbles.

4. Set the soap aside for at least 2 hours to cool and harden. Remove soap from the mold after it has fully hardened.

Cranberry Vanilla Soap

This soap has a soft vanilla scent. The dried cranberries give it some holiday feel.

Ingredients

- 1 lb. shea melt-and-pour soap base

- ¼ cup dried cranberries

- 0.04 oz. (20 drops) vanilla soap fragrance

Instructions

1. Divide the dried cranberries evenly between the cavities of your mold. Set aside.

2. Cut the soap base into small cubes and place them in a microwave-safe bowl. Melt them in the microwave in 30-second increments, stirring in between each burst.

3. Once the soap base has completely melted, stir in the essential oil. Mix thoroughly.

4. Pour the melted soap into your prepared mold. Lightly spray the soap with alcohol to get rid of bubbles.

5. Set the soap aside for at least 2 hours to cool and harden before removing from the mold.

Earl Grey Tea Soap

Infused with citrus essential oils, this melt-and-pour soap smells wonderful. This recipe uses a triple butter soap base, giving the soap a lovely lather.

Ingredients

- 2 lbs. triple butter melt-and-pour soap base

- 0.16 oz. (1 tsp.) bergamot essential oil

- 0.08 oz. (½ tsp.) Litsea cubeba essential oil

- 0.08 oz. (½ tsp.) sweet orange essential oil

- 2 tea bags of earl grey tea

Instructions

1. Cut the soap base into small chunks and place them in a microwave-safe bowl. Melt the soap in the microwave using 30-second intervals, stirring in between.

2. Once the soap base has completely melted, add 1 bag of tea and mix thoroughly. Stir in the essential oils and mix until they're fully dispersed.

3. Pour the soap mixture into your prepared mold. Spritz some alcohol on the surface if there are bubbles on your soap. Sprinkle the other bag of tea evenly on top of the soap.

4. Set the soap aside for 2 to 4 hours to cool and harden. When the soap has fully hardened, remove it from the mold and slice into bars, if necessary.

Flower Cupcake Soap

These flower cupcake soaps are made easy using melt-and-pour soap base. You won't need to add color to make them look stunning but you can definitely use some light colorant if you want to. For this recipe, you'll have to use small paper or silicone cupcake cases to shape the soap.

Ingredients

- 1 lb. white melt-and-pour soap base

- 0.4 oz. (2.5 tsp.) fragrance oil

- dried rose petals

Instructions

1. Chop the soap base into small pieces and place them in a microwave-safe dish. Microwave the soap base in 30-second increments, stirring after each interval.

2. Once the soap base has fully melted, add the fragrance oil and mix thoroughly. Pour soap into the cupcake cases, leaving about ½" of a gap at the top. Make sure that you leave enough soap for the top layer.

3. Set the soap aside to harden slightly so the petals won't sink when they're added. Once the tops are firm enough to hold a thin layer of soap, lightly spray each with alcohol. Add some soap to each cupcake case and sprinkle with the dried petals.

4. Allow the soaps to completely dry for a few hours before removing them from the case.

Gingerbread Soap

This easy-to-make soap is a great homemade holiday gift. For this recipe, you need a 6-cavity gingerbread man mold.

Ingredients

- 16 oz. white melt-and-pour soap base

- 0.25 oz. (½ tbsp.) gingerbread fragrance oil

- brown sparkle color bar

Instructions

1. Chop the soap base into small chunks. Melt the soap in the microwave using 30-second bursts, stirring in between.

2. Once melted, add a small amount of the color bar and mix thoroughly. Add more in small amounts until you're satisfied with the color.

3. Add the fragrance oil and stir until fully dispersed.

4. Pour the soap mixture into your prepared mold. Spray soap with alcohol if there are bubbles. Set aside to cool and harden. Remove from the mold after the soap has fully hardened.

Goat's Milk Lemon Soap

Here's a simple recipe that you and your kids will enjoy making.

Ingredients

- 2 lbs. goat's milk melt-and-pour soap base

- 0.5 oz. (3 tsp.) lemon essential oil

- lemon (or another citrus, like lime and orange)

Instructions

1. Choose lemon that's small enough to fit the size of your mold. Slice it into 1/8" rounds. Place a wire rack on a pan and lay the slices on top of it. Leave it inside your oven preheated to 200°F for 2 to 3 hours or until the lemon is dry. Remove the dried slices and set them aside to cool.

2. Cut the goat's milk soap base into small pieces and place them in a microwave-safe container. Microwave at 30-second intervals, stirring in between. Once the soap is completely melted, add the essential oil and stir.

3. While the soap base is in the microwave, lay out the dried lemon slices inside the cavities of your mold.

4. Quickly pour the melted soap into the mold. After a few hours, pop the soap out of the mold.

Grapefruit Soap with Himalayan Salt

Here's a quick and easy way to incorporate Himalayan salt into your soap. This recipe is so simple it only requires 3 ingredients.

Ingredients

- 1 lb. goat's milk melt-and-pour soap base

- 0.04 oz. (¼ tsp.) grapefruit essential oil

- ¼ cup pink Himalayan salt

Instructions

1. Cut the soap base into small chunks and place them in a microwave-safe bowl. Melt the soap in 30-second intervals, stirring in between.

2. Once the soap base has completely melted, stir in the essential oil. Add the Himalayan salt and mix until they're evenly dispersed.

3. Pour the soap mixture into the cavities of your prepared mold. Lightly spray with alcohol to get rid of bubbles.

4. Set the soap aside for at least 2 hours to cool and harden before removing them from the mold.

Honey and Oatmeal Soap

This simple recipe is perfect for all beginners. It's quite easy to make and the ingredients are easily accessible if you don't have them yet in your kitchen.

Ingredients

- 1 lb. Castile or glycerin melt-and-pour soap base

- ½ oz. 100% pure honey

- 4 tbsp. steel-cut oatmeal

Instructions

1. Cut the soap base into small cubes and place them in a stockpot or a large saucepan. Using a stove burner, melt the soap over medium heat. Stir once in a while until soap is fully melted but don't allow it to boil. Remove pan from heat.

2. Place the honey in a small microwave-safe bowl. Put it in the microwave on high for 15 seconds. Immediately pour the heated honey into the melted soap base and stir until the two ingredients are combined well.

3. Add oatmeal to the mixture. Stir until oats are evenly distributed.

4. Pour the soap mixture into the cavities of your prepared mold. Spritz some alcohol on the surface if there are bubbles forming on your soap.

5. Set the soap aside for 2 to 4 hours to cool and harden before removing them from the mold.

Honeysuckle Soap

This soap recipe will allow you to enjoy the scent of honeysuckle year round. The turmeric powder gives this soap a natural color.

Ingredients

- 2 lbs. baby buttermilk melt-and-pour soap base

- 0.75 oz. (4.5 tsp.) wild honeysuckle fragrance oil

- ½ tsp. turmeric powder

- 0.1 oz. vitamin E oil (optional)

Instructions

1. Chop the soap base into small chunks. Melt them in the microwave. Don't forget to stir every 30 seconds.

2. Once melted, add the turmeric powder and mix until fully incorporated. Make sure no clumps of powder remain.

3. Stir in the fragrance oil and vitamin E oil. Mix thoroughly.

4. Pour the soap into your prepared mold. If there are any bubbles, lightly spray the soap with isopropyl alcohol.

5. Set the soap aside to cool and harden. After about 2 hours, remove soap from the mold.

Lemon Poppy Seed Soap

The soap base for this recipe is infused with 3 kinds of butter—mango, shea, and cocoa. But this recipe will work with any kind of soap base.

Ingredients

- 1 lb. triple butter melt-and-pour soap base

- 0.16 oz. (1 tsp.) lemon fragrance oil

- 2 tbsp. poppy seeds

- ½ tsp. yellow soap colorant

Instructions

1. Using a kitchen knife, cut the soap base into small cubes and place them in a microwave-safe bowl. Melt the cubes in the microwave using 30-second intervals. Stir soap between each interval.

2. Once soap base has completely melted, add the colorant a few drops at a time and stir thoroughly until the color is completely incorporated and you've achieved the tone you want.

3. Stir in the fragrance oil and mix to disperse. Add the poppy seeds and stir thoroughly. You can use less or more seeds depending on how you want your soap to look.

4. Pour soap into the loaf mold. Continue stirring until it thickens to keep the seeds from settling at the bottom. Set aside for a couple of hours to cool and harden.

5. Remove soap from the mold and slice it into bars.

Lime and Cilantro Soap

The combination of lime and cilantro essential oils gives this soap an invigorating scent.

Ingredients

- 1 lb. shea melt-and-pour soap base

- 0.04 oz. (¼ tsp.) lime essential oil

- 0.04 oz. (¼ tsp.) cilantro essential oil

Instructions

1. Cut the soap base into small chunks and place them in a microwave-safe bowl. Microwave in 30-second intervals, stirring after each burst until soap melts completely.

2. Add the essential oils to melted soap. Mix thoroughly.

3. Pour soap in the cavities of your prepared mold. If there are bubbles, spray the soap with isopropyl alcohol.

4. Allow soap to cool and harden for about 2 hours before removing from the mold.

Lemon and Raspberry Soap

Here's another simple recipe that you should try if you love the smell of citrus and raspberry. The added shea butter makes this soap extra-moisturizing.

Ingredients

- 1 lb. goat's milk melt-and-pour soap base

- 0.5 oz. (1 tbsp.) shea butter

- 0.08 (½ tsp.) lemon essential oil

- 0.08 (½ tsp.) raspberry essential oil

Instructions

1. Cut the soap base into small cubes. Melt the soap in the microwave, stirring after every 30 seconds.

2. Melt the shea butter in a separate container using 10-seconds bursts. Once melted, add it to the soap base.

3. Stir in the essential oils. Mix until they're fully dispersed.

4. Pour the soap mixture into your prepared mold. Spray soap with alcohol if there are bubbles. Set aside to cool and harden.

5. After about 2 hours or when the soap has fully hardened, remove it from the mold.

Lemongrass Soap

This recipe combines the healing properties of eucalyptus and the uplifting scent of lemongrass. Matcha powder gives the soap a natural green color.

Ingredients

- 1 lb. glycerin melt-and-pour soap base

- 0.5 oz. (1 tbsp.) shea butter

- 0.16 oz. (1 tsp.) lemongrass essential oil

- 0.08 oz. (½ tsp.) eucalyptus essential oil

- 0.08 oz. (½ tsp.) cedarwood essential oil

- 1 tsp. matcha powder

Instructions

1. Cut the soap base into small chunks and place them in a microwave-safe bowl. Melt the soap in 30-second intervals, stirring in between. Once melted, add the shea butter and heat until it melts.

2. Add matcha powder to the melted soap and mix until it completely dissolves into the soap. Stir in the essential oil and mix to disperse.

3. Pour the soap mixture into your prepared mold. Lightly spray with alcohol if there are bubbles.

4. Set the soap aside for at least 2 hours. Remove soap from the mold after it has completely hardened.

Milk and Honey Soap

This quick-and-easy recipe creates a soap that offers lots of skin benefits. To make your soap look unique, use a silicone honeycomb mold.

Ingredients

- 1 lb. goat's milk melt-and-pour soap base

- 2.25 oz. raw honey

- liquid soap colorant (optional)

Instructions

1. Slice the soap base into small cubes using a kitchen knife. Place the cubes in a microwave-safe container. Cover the container to keep the soap from drying out.

2. Melt the soap in the microwave with 30-second intervals, stirring after each increment. Make sure soap is completely melted before proceeding to the next step.

3. Stir in raw honey and a few drops of the colorant of your choice.

4. Pour soap mixture into the mold and set aside for at least two hours.

5. When the soap has completely hardened and cooled, remove it from the mold.

Orange and Bergamot Soap

This recipe uses essential oils that give the soap a soothing and sweet smell. Paprika gives it a natural orange color.

Ingredients

- 1 lb. white melt-and-pour soap base

- 1 tsp. paprika powder

- 0.16 oz. (1 tsp.) bergamot essential oil

- 0.16 oz. (1 tsp.) sweet orange essential oil

- 0.04 oz. (¼ tsp.) frankincense essential oil

Instructions

1. Cut the soap base into small cubes and place them in a microwave-safe bowl. Melt the soap in 30-second intervals, stirring in between each burst.

2. Once the soap base has completely melted, add the paprika powder. Mix until fully dissolved and the color is evenly dispersed. Stir in the essential oils and mix thoroughly.

3. Pour the soap mixture into your prepared mold. Lightly spray with isopropyl alcohol to get rid of bubbles.

4. Set the soap aside for at least 2 hours to cool and harden before removing from the mold.

Orange Turmeric Soap

This beginner-friendly recipe uses turmeric to give color to the soap. The orange scent perfectly complements the natural orange color.

Ingredients

- 2 lbs. goat's milk melt-and-pour soap base

- 1 tsp. turmeric powder

- 0.4 oz. (2.5 tsp.) orange essential oil

- 1 tbsp. 99% isopropyl alcohol

Instructions

1. Combine the turmeric powder and isopropyl alcohol and mix. This helps the turmeric powder disperse into the soap without lumps. Set aside.

2. Cut the soap base into small cubes and place them in a microwave-safe bowl. Melt the soap in the microwave using 30-second intervals, stirring between each burst.

3. Once the soap base has completely melted, stir in the essential oil and dispersed turmeric. Mix thoroughly.

4. Pour the soap mixture into a 6-cavity rectangular mold. Lightly spray the top of each bar with isopropyl alcohol if there are bubbles.

5. Set the soap aside for at least 2 hours to cool and harden. When the soap has fully hardened, remove the bars from the mold.

Patchouli Charcoal Soap

If you want a detoxifying facial soap, you can easily make one with this recipe.

Ingredients

- 1.5 oz. shea butter melt-and-pour soap base

- 2 tbsp. activated charcoal powder

- 0.16 oz. (1 tsp.) patchouli essential oil

Instructions

1. Cut the soap base into small cubes and melt them in the microwave in 30-second intervals. Stir soap in between each burst.

2. Once the soap base has completely melted, add the activated charcoal powder. Mix until the color is evenly dispersed and no clumps of charcoal remain. Stir in the essential oil and mix thoroughly.

3. Pour the soap mixture into your prepared mold. If there are any bubbles, lightly spray the soap with isopropyl alcohol.

4. Set the soap aside for at least 2 hours to cool and harden before removing from the mold.

Pumpkin Spice Soap

This recipe is for a lightly colored soap. If you want your soap to have a brighter color, feel free to add a few more drops of colorant.

Ingredients

- 2 lbs. shea butter melt-and-pour soap base

- 2 tbsp. pumpkin pie spice

- 4 drops yellow colorant

- 2 drops red colorant

Instructions

1. Cut the soap base into small chunks and place them in a microwave-safe bowl. Melt the soap in 30-second intervals, stirring in between.

2. Once the soap base has completely melted, stir in the pumpkin pie spice and colorant. Mix until they're fully dispersed.

3. Pour the soap mixture into your prepared mold. If there are bubbles forming on your soap, lightly spray it with alcohol.

4. Set the soap aside for at least 2 hours to cool and harden. When the soap has fully hardened, remove it from the mold and slice into bars.

Rose Loofah Soap

Loofah soaps naturally exfoliate, allowing moisture to fully nourish the skin. They make great handmade gifts for many occasions. For this project, you need to find a mold that's big enough to fit the loofah.

Ingredients

- 1 lb. goat's milk or avocado melt-and-pour soap base

- 0.03 oz. (15 drops) rose essential oil

- ½ tsp. rose mica powder

- 1 natural loofah

Instructions

1. Cut loofah into 1" rounds. If you want the loofah completely inside your soap, make thinner slices. Place the slices in the mold.

2. Mix mica powder with a small amount of alcohol. Set aside.

3. Break the soap base into small chunks and place them in a microwave-safe bowl. Microwave on 30-second intervals until soap is completely melted, stirring in between intervals.

4. Add the mica to the melted soap. Continue to mix until color is evenly dispersed. Stir in the essential oil.

5. Pour soap in the mold. If there are bubbles forming, spray it lightly with isopropyl alcohol. Set aside.

6. Remove the soap from the mold after a couple of hours.

Spiced Apple Soap

This simple soap recipe uses apple spice and fragrance oil for a lovely scent of fall.

Ingredients

- 1 lb. goat's milk melt-and-pour soap base

- 0.16 oz. (1 tsp.) Apple fragrance oil

- ½ tsp. apple pie spice

- orange liquid soap colorant

Instructions

1. Cut the soap base into small chunks and place them in a microwave-safe bowl. Melt soap in the microwave using 30-second intervals, stirring after each burst.

2. Once melted, stir in the apple pie spice and essential oil. Add 2 drops of orange colorant and mix thoroughly.

3. Pour soap into your prepared mold. If you see any bubbles, spray the soap with isopropyl alcohol to get rid of them.

4. Set aside for about 2 hours. Release the soap bars from the mold after they have completely hardened.

Sweet Almond Soap

This simple recipe makes a mildly-scented soap that softens and lightly exfoliates the skin.

Ingredients

- 1 lb. shea butter melt-and-pour soap base

- 0.16 oz. (1 tsp.) sweet almond fragrance oil

- 1 tbsp. poppy seeds

Instructions

1. Cut the soap base into small chunks and place them in a microwave-safe bowl. Melt the soap in 30-second intervals, stirring in between.

2. Once the soap base has completely melted, stir in the essential oil and poppy seeds. Mix until they're fully dispersed.

3. Pour the soap mixture into your prepared mold. If there are bubbles, lightly spray the soap with alcohol.

4. Set the soap aside for at least 2 hours to cool and harden. Pop the soap out of the mold after it has fully hardened.

Vanilla Latte Soap

Love coffee? This soap recipe is for you.

Ingredients

- 1 lb. goat's milk melt-and-pour soap base

- coffee grounds (for 1 cup of coffee)

- vanilla essential oil

Instructions

1. Brew a cup of coffee. Set aside both coffee and grounds.

2. Cut the soap base into small chunks and place them in a microwave-safe bowl. Place the bowl in the microwave and melt the soap in 30-second intervals, stirring in between.

3. Once the soap base has completely melted, add the coffee grounds, a ¼ cup of the brewed coffee, and a few drops of essential oil. Mix until they're fully dispersed.

4. Pour the soap mixture into your prepared mold. If there are bubbles forming on your soap, lightly spray it with alcohol.

5. Set the soap aside for at least 2 hours to cool and harden. When the soap bars have fully hardened, remove them from the mold.

White Tea and Ginger Loofah Soap

Here's another loofah soap recipe, but this time it has a white tea and ginger scent. You may also want to use a round silicone soap mold that's about the size of your loofah.

Ingredients

- 1 lb. detergent-free glycerin melt-and-pour soap base

- 0.4 oz. (3 tsp.) white tea and ginger fragrance oil

- liquid soap colorant (optional)

- 1 loofah

Instructions

1. Using a bread knife, slice the loofah into 1" rounds. Place the loofah rounds into each cavity of the mold.

2. Cut the soap base into small cubes using a kitchen knife. Place the cubes in a Pyrex measuring cup and microwave in 30-second increments until soap has fully melted, stirring in between.

3. Stir fragrance oil into the soap base. Add the liquid colorant a few drops at a time and mix until color is fully incorporated and you're satisfied with the hue.

4. Pour the soap into the cavities of your mold. The loofah will absorb some of the melted soap so you'll have to pour more soap until each cavity is filled completely.

5. Set the soap aside for a few hours to harden. When it's hard enough, pop each soap out of the mold.

Cold-Process Soap Recipes

Castile Soap

Castile soaps are made purely with . It's so easy to make but the soap will take a lot more time to completely harden.

Ingredients

- 16 oz. olive oil

- 4.8 oz. distilled water

- 2.06 oz. lye

- ½ oz. sodium lactate (optional)

Instructions

1. Place the water in a heat-proof container. Slowly add the lye and stir until it has totally dissolved. Set aside and allow the solution to cool to around 110°F. Stir in sodium lactate when the temperature reaches below 130°F.

2. Heat the olive oil up to around 110°F in the microwave or in a pot over low heat.

3. Once the right temperature is reached, carefully pour the lye solution to the olive oil. Blend using a stick blender. Alternate between manually stirring and pulsing, then bring the mixture to a medium trace. This will take several minutes.

4. Pour the soap batter into your prepared mold. Cover the mold with a piece of cardboard and towel to insulate the soap.

5. After 24 to 48 hours, check if the soap has completely hardened. If not, give it more time in the mold but without the cover. Once the soap is firm enough, remove it from the mold. Cut into bars, if necessary. Allow soap to cure for 4 to 6 weeks.

Coconut Soap

Requiring only three ingredients, this is definitely among the simplest soap recipes. It's the perfect recipe if you want to try making cold-process soap.

Ingredients

- 33 oz. coconut oil

- 9.6 oz. water

- 4.83 oz. lye

- 0.8 oz. fragrance oil (optional)

Instructions

1. Place cold water in a heat-proof container. Slowly add the lye and stir until it has totally dissolved. Set aside and allow the solution to cool.

2. Melt coconut oil in a large pan over low heat. Once it has melted, remove from heat and allow to cool.

3. Once the temperatures are at 100-110°F, carefully pour the lye solution to the melted coconut oil. Blend using a stick blender, alternating between manually mixing and pulsing. If you're adding fragrance oil, bring the mixture to a light trace. Otherwise, blend to a medium trace.

4. Add the fragrance or essential oil of your choice to the soap mixture. Blend until completely mixed and bring the mixture to a medium trace.

5. Pour soap mixture into your prepared mold. Cover the mold with a piece of cardboard and insulate the soap by covering it with a towel.

6. If your soap needs to be cut into bars, remove it from the mold once it has cooled and hardened. Don't wait for 24 hours or it will be too hard to cut. Allow the bars to cure for 2 to 3 weeks.

Lard Soap

If it's your first time making a cold-process soap, this is the perfect recipe. It uses 100% lard, which is cheap and easy to find.

Ingredients

- 2 lbs. lard

- 12.16 oz. distilled water

- 4.25 oz. lye

- 0.8 oz. fragrance oil (optional)

Instructions

1. Place the water in a heatproof container. Slowly add the lye and stir until it has totally dissolved. Set aside and allow the solution to cool to 110-120°F.

2. Melt the lard in a large pan over low heat. Once melted, remove from heat and allow to cool to 110-120°F.

3. Once the right temperature is reached, carefully pour the lye solution to the melted lard. Blend using a stick blender. Alternate between manually stirring and pulsing and bring the mixture to a light trace.

4. Stir in the fragrance oil, if using. Continue blending until the batter reaches a medium trace.

5. Pour the soap batter into the prepared mold. Insulate the soap for 24 hours by covering the mold with a piece of cardboard and towel.

6. Once the soap is firm enough, remove it from the mold. Cut soap into bars and let them cure for 4 to 6 weeks.

Basic Tallow Soap

Tallow is fat derived from cattle. Like lard, it's inexpensive and easy to find.

Ingredients

- 8 oz. tallow

- 4 oz. coconut oil

- 4 oz. olive oil

- 6.08 oz. water

- 2.27 oz. lye

Instructions

1. Place water in a heat-proof container. Slowly add the lye and stir until it completely dissolves. Set aside and allow the solution to cool to 110-120°F.

2. Melt tallow and coconut oil in a large pan over low heat. Once melted, add the olive oil. Remove from heat and allow to cool to 110-120°F.

3. Once the two mixtures reach the right temperature, carefully pour the lye solution into the oil mix. Blend using a stick blender. Alternate between manually stirring and pulsing, then bring the mixture to a medium trace.

4. Pour the soap batter into your prepared mold. Insulate the soap for 24 hours by covering the mold with a piece of cardboard and towel.

5. Remove soap from the mold and slice into bars. Allow bars to cure for 4 to 6 weeks.

Tallow Soap with Honey

This is a variation of the basic tallow soap recipe. The added honey imparts a light, sweet scent and helps increase the lather.

Ingredients

- 20 oz. tallow

- 4 oz. coconut oil

- 1 oz. honey

- 9.12 oz. distilled water

- 3.41 oz. lye

Instructions

1. Place water in a heatproof container. Slowly add the lye and stir until it has totally dissolved. Set aside and allow the solution to cool (100-110°F).

2. Place tallow and coconut oil in a pot over low heat. Once both are completely melted, add the honey. Remove from heat and allow to cool to 100-110°F.

3. Once the two mixtures reach the right temperature, carefully pour the lye solution into the oil mix. Blend using a stick blender. Alternate between manual stirring and pulsing until the mixture reaches a medium trace.

4. Pour soap mixture into your prepared mold and allow it to cool and harden. After 24 hours, remove soap from the mold and slice it into bars. Cure the soap bars for at least 4 weeks.

Basic Cold-Process Soap

Here's another cold process soap recipe that's great for beginners. It only requires 5 ingredients and the oils make the soap harden relatively fast.

Ingredients

- 26 oz. olive oil

- 6 oz. coconut oil

- 1 oz. castor oil

- 10 oz. water

- 4.4 oz. lye

Instructions

1. Place the water in a glass or sturdy plastic jug. Slowly add the lye and stir until it has totally dissolved. Set aside and allow the solution to cool.

2. Place the olive oil, coconut oil, and castor oil in a large pan and melt them over low heat. Remove from heat and allow to cool.

3. Once the temperatures of the two mixtures are at 90-100°F, carefully pour the lye solution to the oil mix. Blend using a stick blender and bring the mixture to a medium trace.

4. Pour soap mixture into the mold. If bubbles have formed, lightly spray the top with isopropyl alcohol to remove them.

5. Insulate the soap for 24 hours by covering the mold with a piece of cardboard and towel. Once it's firm enough, remove soap from the mold and let them cure for 3 to 4 weeks.

Basic Vegan Soap

Many handmade soap recipes include animal-based ingredients but it's not difficult to make a plant-based soap that's just as good. Here's a simple recipe for a cruelty-free soap.

Ingredients

- 16 oz. palm oil

- 16 oz. coconut oil

- 13.5 oz. olive oil

- 16 oz. water

- 6.5oz. lye

- 1 oz. fragrance or essential oil (optional)

Instructions

1. Place cooled water in a glass or sturdy plastic jug. Slowly add the lye and stir until it has totally dissolved. Set aside and allow the solution to cool.

2. Place the olive oil, coconut oil, and palm oil in a large pan and melt them over low heat. Once solid oils have melted, remove from heat and allow to cool.

3. Once the temperatures of the two mixtures are at 90-100°F, carefully pour the lye solution into the oil mix. Blend using a stick blender and bring the mixture to a light trace.

4. Add the fragrance or essential oil of your choice to the soap mixture. Blend until completely mixed and bring the mixture to a medium trace.

5. Pour soap mixture into the mold. Insulate the soap for 24 to 48 hours by covering the mold with a piece of cardboard and towel.

Once it's firm enough, remove soap from the mold and let them cure for 3 to 4 weeks.

Bastille Soap

This recipe creates a soap with the same mildness as castile soap. It makes use of other oils to save some time. Colorful dried flowers are added, making them look more attractive.

Ingredients

- 20 oz. olive oil

- 2.5 oz. palm oil

- 2.5 oz. coconut oil

- 8 oz. water

- 3.25 oz. lye

- 0.5 oz. lavender fragrance oil (optional)

- dried lavender flowers (optional)

Instructions

1. Slowly add the lye to the water and stir until the lye has totally dissolved. Set aside and allow the solution to cool to 100-110°F.

2. Place the olive oil, coconut oil, and palm oil in a large pan over low heat. Remove from heat when solid oils have melted and allow to cool.

3. Once the temperatures of the two mixture are within 10° of each other, carefully pour the lye solution into the oil mix. Blend using a stick blender and bring the mixture to a light trace.

4. Stir in the fragrance oil with the stick blender and blend until completely mixed. Bring the mixture to a medium trace.

5. Pour soap mixture into the mold. Remove any bubbles and prevent soda ash from forming by lightly spraying the top with 99% isopropyl alcohol.

6. Insulate the soap for 24 hours by covering the mold with a sheet of wax paper and a towel. Once it's firm enough, remove soap from the mold. If you're using a loaf mold, cut your soap into bars. Firmly press the top of each soap into the dried flowers and shake off any loose petals. Cure the soap bars for at least 4 weeks.

Supermarket Soap

This cold-process soap requires 4 oils, which you can easily find in any supermarket.

Ingredients

- 7.5 oz. olive oil

- 6.5 oz. palm oil

- 6.5 oz. coconut oil

- 1.3 oz. castor oil

- 8 oz. water

- 3.1 oz. lye

- 0.5 oz. fragrance or essential oil (optional)

Instructions

1. Place the water in a heatproof container. Slowly add the lye and stir until it has completely dissolved. Set aside and allow the solution to cool.

2. Place the coconut oil and palm oil in a pot over low heat. Once melted, add the olive oil and castor oil. Remove from heat and allow the mixture to cool.

3. Once the temperatures of the two mixtures reach 100-110°F, carefully pour the lye solution into the oil mix. Blend using a stick blender. Alternate between pulsing and manually stirring until the mixture reaches a light trace.

4. Stir in the fragrance oil and bring the mixture to a medium trace.

5. Pour the soap batter into your prepared mold. Insulate soap by covering the mold with a piece of cardboard and a towel. After 24

hours or when it has fully hardened, release it from the mold. Cut the soap into bars and let them cure for around 4 weeks.

Supermarket Soap with Shea Butter

This recipe uses 3 easy-to-find oils. The addition of shea butter makes the soap extra hydrating.

Ingredients

- 4.8 oz. olive oil

- 4.8 oz. coconut oil

- 3.2 oz. palm oil

- 3.2 oz. shea butter

- 6 oz. water

- 2.2 oz. lye

- 0.4 oz. fragrance or essential oil (optional)

Instructions

1. Place water in a heatproof container. Slowly add the lye and stir until it completely dissolves. Set aside and allow the solution to cool.

2. Place the coconut oil, palm oil, and shea butter in a pot over low heat. Once melted, add the olive oil. Remove from heat and allow the mixture to cool.

3. Once the temperatures of the two mixtures reach 100-110°F, carefully pour the lye solution into the oil mix. Blend using a stick blender. Alternate between pulsing and manually stirring until the mixture reaches a light trace.

4. Stir in the fragrance oil and bring the mixture to a medium trace.

5. Pour the soap batter into the cavities of your mold. Cover the mold with a piece of cardboard and a towel to insulate soap. After

at least 24 hours, release the soap from the mold and cure for 4 to 6 weeks.

Lavender Soap

This simple soap recipe uses lavender essential oil for a soothing and relaxing scent.

Ingredients

- 14 oz. olive oil pomace

- 7 oz. coconut oil

- 7 oz. palm oil

- 10.64 oz. distilled water

- 3.94 lye

- 0.75 oz. lavender essential oil

Instructions

1. Place the water in a heatproof container. Slowly add the lye and stir until it has completely dissolved. Set aside and allow the solution to cool.

2. Place the coconut oil and palm oil in a pot over low heat. Once melted, add the olive oil. Remove from heat and allow the mixture to cool.

3. Once the temperatures of the two mixtures reach 100-110°F, carefully pour the lye solution into the oil mix. Blend using a stick blender. Alternate between pulsing and manually stirring until the mixture reaches a light trace.

4. Stir in the essential oil and bring the mixture to a medium trace.

5. Pour the soap batter into your prepared mold. Insulate soap by covering the mold with a piece of cardboard and a towel for 24 to 48 hours. Remove from the mold then cut into bars, if necessary. Allow the soap to cure for around 4 weeks.

Chapter 3
Beauty Recipes

Body Soap Recipes

Avocado and Yogurt Soap

Avocado and yogurt make this soap feels silky and extra moisturizing. The spirulina powder gives it a natural green color.

Ingredients

- 19.8 oz. palm oil

- 9 oz. rice bran oil

- 7.2 oz. refined coconut oil

- 7.3 oz. distilled water

- 4.9 oz. lye

- 3 oz. avocado puree (from ripe avocado)

- 2 oz. plain Greek yogurt

- 1 tbsp. spirulina powder

Instructions

1. Place the water in a heatproof container. Slowly add the lye and stir until it has completely dissolved. Set aside and allow the solution to cool to 90-100°F.

2. Place the coconut oil and palm oil in a pot over low heat. Once melted, add the rice bran oil. Remove from heat and allow the mixture to cool to 90-100°F.

3. Once the two mixtures have reached the right temperature, carefully pour the lye solution into the oil mix. Blend using a stick blender. Alternate between pulsing and manually stirring until the mixture reaches a light trace.

4. Stir in the avocado puree, yogurt, and spirulina powder. Blend and bring the mixture to a medium trace.

5. Pour the soap batter into your prepared loaf mold. Insulate soap by covering the mold with a piece of cardboard and a towel.

6. After at least 24 hours, remove soap from the mold. Cut it into bars and let them cure for 4 to 6 weeks.

Babassu and Olive Soap

Designed to be low-cleansing and extra-conditioning, this is perfect for those who suffer from dry skin.

Ingredients

- 12.8 oz. olive oil
- 2.4 oz. babassu oil
- 0.8 oz. castor oil
- 4.8 oz. distilled water
- 2.1 oz. lye
- 0.5 oz. sodium lactate

Instructions

1. Place the water in a heatproof container. Slowly add the lye and stir until it has completely dissolved. Allow the solution to cool to 90-100°F. Stir in the sodium lactate when the solution's temperature drops to below 130°F.

2. Place the olive oil, babassu oil, and castor oil in a pot over low heat. When no more solid oils are left, remove from heat. Allow the mixture to cool to 90-100°F.

3. Once the two mixtures have reached the right temperature, carefully pour the lye solution into the oil mix. Blend using a stick blender. Alternate between pulsing and manually stirring until the mixture reaches a medium trace.

4. Pour the soap batter into the cavities of your mold. Cover the mold with cardboard and towel to insulate the soap. After 24 to 48 hours, check to see if your soap is ready to be unmolded. If

not, remove the covers and give the soap a couple more days to harden.

5. Release soap bars from the mold and allow them to cure for at least 4 weeks.

Banana and Yogurt Soap

This moisturizing soap contains banana powder, which is great for dry skin. It also has flax seed oil that's rich in fatty acids believed to promote youthful skin.

Ingredients

- 17.6 oz. olive oil

- 4.8 oz. babassu oil

- 3.2 oz. cocoa butter

- 1.6 oz. shea butter

- 1.6 oz. refined coconut oil

- 1.6 oz. castor oil

- 1.6 oz. flax seed oil

- 9.75 oz. distilled water

- 4.25 oz. lye

- 1 oz. sodium lactate (60% solution)

- 0.6 oz. banana powder

- 0.4 oz. yogurt powder

- 0.9 oz. fragrance or essential oil (optional)

Instructions

1. Place the water in a heatproof container. Slowly add the lye and stir until it has completely dissolved. Set aside and allow the solution to cool to around 100°F. Add sodium lactate when the solution's temperature is below 130°F.

2. Place the coconut oil, babassu oil, cocoa butter, and shea butter in a pot over low heat. Once melted, add the olive oil, castor oil, and flaxseed oil. Remove from heat and allow the mixture to cool to around 100°F.

3. Once the two mixtures have reached the right temperature, carefully pour the lye solution to the oil mix. Add the banana powder and yogurt powder. Blend using a stick blender, alternating between pulsing and manually stirring. Bring the mixture to a medium trace. If you're using fragrance or essential oil, add it when the mixture reaches a light trace.

4. Pour the soap batter into your prepared mold. Cover the mold with a sheet of wax paper or cardboard. Insulate the soap for 24 to 48 hours by covering it with a towel.

5. Check to see if the soap is firm enough. If not, give it more time to harden.

6. Remove soap from the mold and slice it into bars. Allow them to cure for 4 to 6 weeks before using.

Calendula Soap with Litsea Cubeba

Calendula and Litsea cubeba are known to help in treating skin problems. Calendula is also one of the few flowers that retain their color when mixed with lye in soap making.

Ingredients

- 14 oz. olive oil

- 7 oz. coconut oil

- 5 oz. shea butter

- 1.76 oz. castor oil

- 7 oz. water

- 3.8 oz. lye

- 0.65 oz. Litsea cubeba essential oil

- 2 tsp. dried calendula petals

Instructions

1. Place the water in a heatproof container. Slowly add the lye and stir. Once it has completely dissolved, add the calendula petals. Stir a bit and set aside. Allow the solution to cool to 100-110°F.

2. Place the coconut oil and shea butter in a pot over low heat. Once melted, remove the pot from heat and add the olive oil and castor oil. Allow the mixture to cool to 100-110°F.

3. Once the two mixtures have reached the right temperature, carefully pour the lye solution to the oil mix. Blend using a stick blender. Alternate between pulsing and manually stirring until the mixture reaches a light trace.

4. Stir in the essential oil and bring the mixture to a medium trace.

5. Pour the soap batter into your prepared mold. Cover the mold with a sheet of wax paper or cardboard. Insulate the soap for 24 to 48 hours by covering it with a towel.

6. Remove the soap from the mold once it's firm enough. Slice it into bars and let them cure for 4 to 6 weeks.

Carrot Soap

This recipe uses fresh carrots to make a soap that's great for your skin. Carrots are rich in anti-oxidants and beta-carotene, which are believed to give the skin additional protection.

Ingredients

- 14 oz. palm oil

- 10 oz. coconut oil

- 8 oz. olive oil

- 6.32 oz. distilled water

- 4.66 oz. lye

- 3 oz. pureed cooked carrot

- 0.5 oz. poppy seeds

Instructions

1. Combine water and carrot puree in a heatproof container. Slowly add the lye and stir until it has completely dissolved. Set aside and allow the solution to cool.

2. Place the coconut oil and palm oil in a pot over low heat. Once melted, add the olive oil. Remove from heat and allow the mixture to cool.

3. Once the temperatures of the two mixtures reach 100-110°F, carefully pour the lye solution into the oil mix. Blend using a stick blender. Alternate between pulsing and manually stirring until the mixture reaches a light trace.

4. Add the poppy seeds and mix to disperse. Bring the mixture to a medium trace.

5. Pour the soap batter into your prepared loaf mold. Insulate soap by covering the mold with a piece of cardboard and a towel. After 24 to 48 hours, remove it from the mold. Cut soap into bars and allow them to cure for 4 to 6 weeks.

Clover and Aloe Soap

The combination of ingredients in this simple recipe makes a soap that's soothing and moisturizing.

Ingredients

- 1 lb. triple butter melt-and-pour soap base

- 0.32 oz. (2 tsp.) clover and aloe fragrance oil

- 2 tsp. aloe vera gel

- 1 tsp. vitamin E (optional)

Instructions

1. Cut the soap base into small cubes and place them in a microwave-safe bowl. Melt the soap in the microwave, stirring after every 30 seconds.

2. Once the soap base has completely melted, stir in the fragrance oil, aloe vera gel, and vitamin E. Mix until they're fully dispersed.

3. Pour the soap mixture into the cavities of your prepared mold. Lightly spray with alcohol to get rid of bubbles.

4. Set aside for at least 2 hours to cool and harden before releasing the soap bars from the mold.

Coconut-Lime Soap

Another moisturizing soap recipe that uses coconut milk, this one adds lime zest and dried coconut to gently exfoliate.

Ingredients

- 7.5 oz. olive oil
- 7.5 oz. coconut oil
- 4 oz. sunflower oil
- 3 oz. safflower oil
- 7 oz. coconut milk (partially frozen)
- 3.12 oz. lye
- 0.5 oz. lime essential oil
- 1-2 tbsp. lime zest
- 1 cup chopped the dried coconut

Instructions

1. Place the partially frozen coconut milk in a heatproof container. Slowly add the lye and gently stir until it completely dissolves. Set aside and allow the solution to cool to 90-100°F.

2. Place the coconut oil in a pot over low heat. Once melted, add the olive oil, sunflower oil, and safflower oil. Remove from heat and allow the mixture to cool to 90-100°F.

3. Once the two mixtures have reached the right temperature, carefully pour the lye solution into the oil mix. Blend using a stick blender. Alternate between pulsing and manually stirring until the mixture reaches a light trace.

4. Add the lime zest and dried coconut. Mix to disperse and then stir in the essential oil. Bring the soap batter to a thick trace.

5. Spoon the soap batter into your prepared loaf mold. Cover the mold with a piece of cardboard and a towel to insulate soap.

6. After 24 to 48 hours, remove soap from the mold. Slice into bars and allow them to cure for 4 to 6 weeks.

Extra-Moisturizing Soap

This recipe uses coconut milk in place of water, making the soap extra creamy, extra moisturizing, and extra bubbly.

Ingredients

- 6.3 oz. olive oil

- 6.3 oz. coconut oil

- 5.2 oz. palm oil

- 2.1 oz. canola oil

- 1 oz. castor oil

- 7.2 oz. coconut milk (partially frozen)

- 3 oz. lye

- 0.5 oz. fragrance oil

Instructions

1. Place the partially frozen coconut milk in a heatproof container. Slowly add the lye and gently stir until it has completely dissolved. During this step, the milk will change color, thicken a bit, and may give off a bad smell. Set aside and allow the solution to cool to 90-100°F.

2. Place the coconut oil and palm oil in a pot over low heat. Once melted, add the olive oil, canola oil, and castor oil. Remove from heat and allow the mixture to cool to 90-100°F.

3. Once the two mixtures have reached the right temperature, carefully pour the lye solution into the oil mix. Blend using a stick blender. Alternate between pulsing and manually stirring until the mixture reaches a light trace.

4. Stir in the fragrance oil and continue blending until the mixture reaches a thick trace. Make sure that the batter has really thickened or pockets of lye will develop in it.

5. Spoon the soap batter into your prepared mold. Insulate the soap by covering the mold with a piece of cardboard and a towel.

6. Remove soap from the mold after at least 24 hours or it has fully hardened. Cut it into bars and let them cure for 4 to 6 weeks.

Extra-Moisturizing Soap with Shea Butter

Ingredients

- 12.8 oz. olive oil

- 6.4 oz. coconut oil

- 4.8 oz. palm oil

- 4.8 oz. shea butter

- 3.2 oz. castor oil

- 7.05 oz. water (chilled)

- 3.42 oz. coconut milk (partially frozen)

- 4.38 oz. lye

Instructions

1. Combine the chilled water and partially frozen coconut milk in a heatproof container. Slowly add the lye and gently stir until it completely dissolves. Set aside and allow the solution to cool to 90-100°F.

2. Place the coconut oil, palm oil, and shea butter in a pot over low heat. Once melted, add the olive oil and castor oil. Remove from heat and allow the mixture to cool to 90-100°F.

3. Once the two mixtures have reached the right temperature, carefully pour the lye solution into the oil mix. Blend using a stick blender. Alternate between pulsing and manually stirring until the mixture reaches a medium-thick trace.

4. Spoon the soap batter into your prepared mold. Cover the mold with a piece of cardboard and towel to insulate soap.

5. After 24 to 48 hours, remove soap from the mold. Slice into bars and allow them to cure for 4 to 6 weeks.

Ginger Mint Soap

Made with gentle ingredients, this soap is a mild cleanser that nourishes and soothes irritated, dry skin.

Ingredients

- 12.8 oz. pomace olive oil

- 6.4 oz. coconut oil

- 6.4 oz. sweet almond oil

- 3.2 oz. cocoa butter

- 1.6 oz. castor oil

- 1.6 oz. black cumin seed oil

- 10.92 oz. water

- 4.4 oz. lye

- 1 oz. ginger mint fragrance oil

- 0.45 oz. French green clay

Instructions

1. Place the water in a heatproof container. Slowly add the lye and stir until it has completely dissolved. Set aside and allow the solution to cool to 90-100°F.

2. Place the coconut oil and cocoa butter in a pot over low heat. Once melted, add the liquid oils (except essential oil). Remove from heat. Add the green clay and mix. Allow the mixture to cool to 90-100°F.

3. Once the two mixtures have reached the right temperature, carefully pour the lye solution into the oil mix. Blend using a stick

blender. Alternate between pulsing and manually stirring until the mixture reaches a light trace.

4. Stir in the essential oil. Blend until the scent is fully incorporated and the mixture reaches a medium trace.

5. Pour the soap batter into your prepared loaf mold. Cover the mold with cardboard and a towel. Insulate the soap for 24 to 48 hours. Release soap from the mold and cut into bars. Cure the soap bars for at least 4 weeks.

Honey and Lavender Soap

The combination of oils in this recipe makes it ideal for those with sensitive skin.

Ingredients

- 16 oz. olive oil

- 1.25 oz. castor oil

- 6 oz. coconut oil

- 0.75 oz. shea butter

- 0.5 oz. beeswax

- 6 oz. water

- 3.32 oz. lye

- 0.75 oz. sodium lactate (optional)

- 0.16 oz. lavender essential oil

- 0.24 oz. raw honey

- 8 drops grapefruit seed extract

Instructions

1. Place water in a heatproof plastic or glass container. Slowly add the lye and stir until it has totally dissolved. Set aside and allow the solution to cool to 100-110°F. If you're using sodium lactate, add it when the solution's temperature is below 130°F.

2. Place the coconut oil, shea butter, and beeswax in a pot over low heat. Once the solid oils have melted, add the olive oil, castor oil, and ½ of the honey. Remove from heat and allow the mixture to cool to 100-110°F.

3. Once the temperatures of the two mixtures are within 10° of each other, carefully pour the lye solution into the oil mix. Blend using a stick blender and alternate between pulsing and manually stirring the soap batter. Bring the mixture to a light trace.

4. Add the lavender oil, grapefruit seed extract, and the remaining honey to the soap mixture. Stir until they're all dispersed and bring the mixture to a medium trace.

5. Pour soap mixture into the mold. Insulate the soap for 24 to 48 hours by covering the mold with a sheet of wax paper or cardboard and towel. Once it's firm enough, remove soap from the mold and allow to cure for 4 to 6 weeks.

Kombucha Soap

Do you like kombucha? If you don't know it yet, this fermented tea works wonders for your skin. This soap has a natural herbal scent but you can definitely add fragrance if you want.

Ingredients

- 12 oz. tallow

- 8 oz. coconut oil

- 5 oz. olive oil

- 4 oz. mango butter

- 4 oz. Argan oil

- 6 oz. water, chilled

- 4.2 oz. lye

- 6.5 oz. kombucha, chilled

Instructions

1. Place the coconut oil, tallow, olive oil, argan oil, and mango butter in a pot over low heat. Once solid oils have melted, remove from heat. Allow the mixture to cool to 100-110°F.

2. Combine the chilled water and kombucha in a heatproof container. Slowly add the lye and stir until it has totally dissolved. Set aside and allow the solution to cool to 100-110°F.

3. Once the two mixtures have reached the right temperature, carefully pour the lye solution into the oil mix. Blend using a stick blender and alternate between pulsing and manually stirring the soap batter. Bring the mixture to a light trace.

4. Pour the soap batter into your prepared mold. Leave it on the counter to cool and harden or place it in the freezer for 24 hours. When the soap is firm enough, remove it from the mold and slice into bars. Cure the bars for 4 to 6 weeks.

Lavender Oatmeal Soap

This simple recipe combines the reparative properties of oatmeal and the calming power of lavender to cure dry, itchy, and sensitive skin. It only requires 4 ingredients and the whole process takes just a few hours to complete.

Ingredients

- 10 oz. goat's milk melt-and-pour soap

- 0.8 oz. quick-cook oats

- 1 tbsp. dried lavender flowers

- 0.04 oz. (¼ tsp.) lavender essential oil

Instructions

1. Cut the soap base into small chunks and place them in a microwave-safe dish. Add the lavender flowers and oats.

2. Microwave the mixture in 30-second intervals until soap base has fully melted, stirring in between.

3. Add the lavender oil and mix until oil is fully incorporated.

4. Pour melted soap into the mold. Set aside for a couple of hours to cool and harden. You can also place soap inside the fridge if you want to reduce the waiting time.

5. When soap bars are firm enough, pop them out of the mold.

Lavender and Fir Needle Soap

This moisturizing soap is great for dry and itchy winter skin.

Ingredients

- 10.4 oz. pomace olive oil

- 3.2 oz. babassu oil

- 1.6 oz. castor oil

- 0.8 oz. coconut oil

- 5.38 oz. distilled water

- 2.15 oz. lye

- 0.2 oz. lavender essential oil

- 0.2 oz. fir needle essential oil

Instructions

1. Place the water in a heatproof container. Slowly add the lye and stir until it has completely dissolved. Set aside and allow the solution to cool to 90-100°F.

2. Place the coconut oil and babassu oil in a pot over low heat. Once melted, add the olive oil and castor oil. Remove from heat and allow the mixture to cool to 90-100°F.

3. Once the two mixtures have reached the right temperature, carefully pour the lye solution into the oil mix. Blend using a stick blender. Alternate between pulsing and manually stirring until the mixture reaches a light trace.

4. Stir in the essential oils. Blend until oils are fully incorporated and the mixture reaches a medium trace.

5. Pour the soap batter into the cavities of your mold. Cover the mold with cardboard and a towel. After 24 to 48 hours, release the soap bars from the mold and allow them to cure for at least 4 weeks.

Lemon and Green Tea Soap

This recipe makes soap that helps in maintaining healthy skin. It's great for fighting acne, too.

Ingredients

- 1 lb. glycerin melt-and-pour soap base

- 0.12 oz. (¾ tsp.) lemon essential oil

- 2 tbsp. matcha powder

Instructions

1. Cut the soap base into small cubes and place them in a microwave-safe bowl. Melt the soap in the microwave in 30-second increments, stirring after each interval.

2. Once soap base has completely melted, stir in the matcha powder and essential oil. Mix until they're fully dispersed.

3. Pour the soap mixture into your prepared mold. Lightly spray the top with alcohol if there are bubbles forming on your soap.

4. Set the soap aside for at least 2 hours to cool and harden. When the soap bars have fully hardened, remove them from the mold.

Luxurious Soap

This recipe uses avocado butter, which is soothing and hydrating. Combined with almond oil, it heals and replenishes the skin, making this soap perfect for getting rid of acne and stretch marks.

Ingredients

- 12 oz. palm oil

- 8 oz. olive oil

- 7 oz. coconut oil

- 2 oz. avocado butter

- 1 oz. sweet almond oil

- 1 oz. shea butter

- 10.2 oz. water

- 4.2 oz. lye

Instructions

1. Place water in a heat-resistant container. Slowly add the lye and stir until it has totally dissolved. Set aside and allow the solution to cool to 100°F.

2. Place the coconut oil, palm oil, avocado butter, and shea butter in a pot over low heat. Once melted, add the olive oil and sweet almond oil. Remove from heat and allow to cool to 100°F.

3. Once the temperatures are within 10° of each other, carefully pour the lye solution into the oil mix. Blend using a stick blender, alternating between manually stirring and pulsing. Bring the mixture to a medium trace.

4. Pour the soap mixture into your prepared loaf mold and cover it with a piece of cardboard and a towel. Insulate for 24 hours.

5. Remove soap from mold and slice into bars. Allow soap bars to cure for at least 4 weeks.

Moisturizing Grapefruit Soap

This recipe is a sustainable alternative to many moisturizing soaps that use palm. But because it contains a large amount of olive oil, it may take more time to harden. The added sodium lactate will help speed up the process.

Ingredients

- 17 oz. olive oil

- 7 oz. coconut oil

- 2 oz. grapeseed oil

- 8.4 oz. water

- 3.6 oz. lye

- 0.5 oz. grapefruit essential oil

- ½ tsp. pink clay

- 0.25 oz. sodium lactate (optional)

Instructions

1. In a ramekin or small bowl, mix the pink clay with 1 tbsp. olive oil. Set aside.

2. Place the water in a heatproof container. Slowly add the lye and stir until it has completely dissolved. Set aside and allow the solution to cool to around 100°F. Add sodium lactate when the solution's temperature is below 130°F.

3. Place the coconut oil in a pot over low heat. Once melted, remove the pot from heat and add the olive oil and grapeseed oil. Allow the mixture to cool to around 100°F.

4. Once the two mixtures have reached the right temperature, carefully pour the lye solution to the oil mix. Blend using a stick blender. Alternate between pulsing and manually stirring until the mixture reaches a light trace.

5. Stir in the essential oil and clay-oil mix. Blend until the color has fully dispersed and the batter has reached a medium trace.

6. Pour the soap batter into your prepared mold. Cover the mold with a sheet of wax paper or cardboard. Insulate the soap for 24 to 48 hours by covering it with a towel.

7. Check to see if the soap is firm enough. If not, give it more time to harden.

8. Remove soap from the mold and slice it into bars. Let them cure for 4 to 6 weeks before using.

Moisturizing Sunflower Soap

This moisturizing soap contains sunflower oil, which has sun-protection and anti-aging properties. It's naturally colored with lemon peel powder. When you make this soap, the batter will be orange but it will lighten after curing.

Ingredients

- 6 oz. olive oil
- 5 oz. coconut oil
- 2.5 oz. cocoa butter
- 2.5 oz. sunflower oil
- 2 oz. rice bran oil
- 5.25 oz. hot water
- 2.5 oz. lye
- ¾ cup dried sunflower petals
- 1 tsp. lemon peel powder

Instructions

1. Place the sunflower petals in a jar and add the hot water. Steep until the water turns yellow. Strain and place the sunflower tea in the fridge to cool.

2. Weigh the sunflower tea into a heatproof container. If it's less than 5.25 oz., just add some cold water. Slowly add the lye and stir until it has completely dissolved. After 20 minutes, stir in the lemon powder and allow the solution to continue cooling.

3. Place the coconut oil and cocoa butter in a pot over low heat. Once melted, add the olive, sunflower, and rice bran oils.

Remove the pot from heat and allow the mixture to cool to around 90-100°F.

4. Once the temperatures of the two mixtures are within 10° of each other, carefully pour the lye solution to the oil mix. Blend using a stick blender. Alternate between pulsing and manually stirring until the mixture reaches a medium trace.

5. Pour the soap batter into a loaf mold or a mold with 6 sunflower-shaped cavities. Leave it on the counter to cool and harden for 2 to 3 days.

6. Remove soap from the mold. If you used a loaf mold, slice it into bars. Allow curing for 4 to 6 weeks.

Sea Salt Soap

For this recipe, it's better to use a rectangular mold instead of loaf mold as the salt will make the soap too hard to cut. Also, avoid using Dead Sea salt.

Ingredients

- 4.8 oz. coconut oil
- 4.8 oz. olive oil
- 4.8 oz. palm kernel oil
- 0.8 oz. shea butter
- 0.8 oz. castor oil
- 6.08 oz. water
- 2.374 oz. lye
- 0.4 oz. essential oil

Instructions

1. Place the water in a heatproof container. Slowly add the lye and stir until it has completely dissolved. Set aside and allow the solution to cool to 100-110°F.

2. Place the solid oils in a pot over low heat. Once melted, add the liquid oils (except essential oil). Remove from heat and allow the mixture to cool to 100-110°F.

3. Once the two mixtures have reached the right temperature, carefully pour the lye solution into the oil mix. Blend using a stick blender. Alternate between pulsing and manually stirring until the mixture reaches a light trace.

4. Stir in the essential oil and add the salt. Blend until they're fully incorporated and the mixture reaches a medium trace.

5. Pour the soap batter into your prepared mold. Insulate soap for 24 to 48 hours by covering the mold with a piece of cardboard and a towel.

6. After the soap bars have fully hardened, release them from the mold and allow them to cure for 4 to 6 weeks.

Sugar Scrub Cubes

Ingredients

- 9 oz. clear melt-and-pour soap base

- 2 oz. cocoa butter

- 0.16 oz. fragrance oil of choice

- 1 lb. sugar

Instructions

1. Chop the soap base into small cubes. Set aside.

2. Melt the cocoa butter in the microwave using 30-second bursts, stirring in between. Once melted, add the soap base and heat until both are completely melted.

3. Add the fragrance oil and mix thoroughly. Add the sugar and quickly stir the mixture with a spoon.

4. Wearing vinyl or latex gloves, use your hands to blend the mixture into a paste.

5. Quickly pour the mixture into the cavities of your prepared mold. Press firmly to force out air.

6. Refrigerate for about an hour or until mixture is firm. Release the sugar cubes from the mold. If you're using a mold with bigger cavities, cut the mixture into cubes before it sets.

Triple Butter Soap with Buttermilk

This soap is made with a combination of skin-nourishing butter and oil. The addition of buttermilk makes it extra moisturizing and creamy.

Ingredients

- 16.5 oz. olive oil

- 7 oz. coconut oil

- 1.5 oz. mango butter

- 1.5 oz. cocoa butter

- 1.5 oz. shea butter

- 1.5 oz. buttermilk powder

- 10.64 oz. distilled water

- 3.9 oz. lye

- 0.9 oz. fragrance or essential oil

Instructions

1. Place the water in a heatproof container. Slowly add the lye and stir until it has completely dissolved. Set aside and allow the solution to cool.

2. Place the butters and coconut oil in a pot over low heat. Once melted, add the olive oil. Remove from heat. Add the buttermilk powder and mix until dissolved. Set aside to cool.

3. Once the temperatures of the two mixtures reach 100-110°F, carefully pour the lye solution into the oil mix. Blend using a stick blender. Alternate between pulsing and manually stirring until the mixture reaches a light trace.

4. Stir in the fragrance oil and bring the mixture to a medium trace.

5. Pour the soap batter into your prepared loaf mold. Insulate soap by covering the mold with a piece of cardboard and a towel.

6. After 24 hours or when the soap has fully hardened, remove it from the mold. Cut into bars and let them cure for around 4 weeks.

Unscented Moisturizing Soap

This recipe combines gentle oils, making a mild soap that softens and smoothens the skin.

Ingredients

- 20 oz. palm oil

- 17 oz. coconut oil

- 16 oz. safflower oil

- 8 oz. olive oil

- 3 oz. sweet almond oil

- 24 oz. distilled water

- 9 oz. lye

Instructions

1. Place all the oils in a large pot and melt under low heat. Remove from heat once all solids have completely melted. Set aside and allow to cool to 100-110°F.

2. Place the water in a stainless steel or plastic container. Slowly add the lye and stir until it has completely dissolved. Allow the solution to cool to 100-110°F.

3. Once the two mixtures are at about the same temperature, add the lye solution to the melted oils. Mix with the stick blender on and off. Bring the mixture to a medium trace.

4. Transfer the soap mixture into your prepared mold and insulate for at least 24 hours to cool and harden. Remove soap from the mold and cure for 4 to 6 weeks.

Yogurt Soap with Lavender and Chamomile

Made with a blend of oils and butters known for their moisturizing properties, this soap is perfect for dry skin. It's also gentle enough so you can use it as a facial soap.

Ingredients

- 10.8 oz. olive oil

- 10.8 oz. palm oil

- 7.2 oz. coconut oil

- 1.8 oz. Argan oil

- 1.8 oz. safflower oil

- 1.8 oz. cocoa butter

- 1.8 oz. shea butter

- 10 oz. distilled water

- 3 oz. plain Greek yogurt

- 0.2 oz. chamomile flower powder

- 0.2 oz. lavender flower powder

Instructions

1. Place the water in a heatproof container. Slowly add the lye and stir until it has completely dissolved. Set aside and allow the solution to cool to around 110°F.

2. Place the solid oils and butters in a pot over low heat. Once melted, add the liquid oils and remove from heat. Allow the mixture to cool to around 110°F.

3. Once the two mixtures have reached the right temperature, carefully pour the lye solution to the oil mix. Blend using a stick blender. Alternate between pulsing and manually stirring until the mixture reaches a light trace.

4. Stir in the yogurt and powders. Blend until the batter reaches a medium trace.

5. Pour the soap batter into your prepared mold. Cover the mold with a sheet of wax paper or cardboard. Insulate the soap for at least 24 hours by covering it with a towel.

6. When the soap has fully hardened, remove it from the mold. Cut soap into bars and allow them to cure for 4 to 6 weeks.

Facial Soap Recipes

Aloe Vera Beauty Soap

This recipe uses aloe gel freshly extracted from aloe vera leaf, designed for a soap that's gentle to your face.

Ingredients

- 6 oz. olive oil

- 3 oz. coconut oil

- 2 oz. shea butter

- 2 oz. sunflower oil

- 2.5 oz. distilled water

- 1.92 oz. lye

- 2 oz. fresh aloe gel

- 1 oz. castor oil

Instructions

1. Slice the aloe leaf into a few pieces. For each piece, run a sharp knife along the edges to separate the gel from the skin. Press the gel out of the leaf with your fingers or a spoon. Place the gel in a blender and process until smooth. Measure out 2 oz. of gel and store the remaining in the fridge. For longer storage, you can freeze it in an ice tray.

2. Place the water in a heavy-duty plastic or stainless steel container. Sprinkle the lye and stir well. Set the lye solution aside and allow to cool for about 30 minutes to 100-120°F.

3. While waiting for the solution to cool down, melt the coconut oil and shea butter. Once melted, add the remaining oils. Remove from heat and blend in the aloe gel using a stick blender.

4. Once the two mixtures are at about the same temperature, carefully pour the lye solution to the oils/aloe mix. With the stick blender, bring the soap mixture to medium trace by manually stirring and blending with short bursts.

5. Pour the soap mixture into your molds and place it in the freezer. After 24 hours, remove soap from the mold and allow to cure for at least 4 weeks before using.

Anti-Acne Foaming Clay Soap

Making a beauty soap doesn't have to be complicated. This 2-ingredient soap is made using the melt-and-pour method, so anyone can make a soap that soothes and clears up skin issues.

Ingredients

- 2 lbs. glycerin melt-and-pour soap base

- 2 oz. bentonite clay

Instructions

1. Break the soap base into small chunks and put them in a microwave-safe bowl. Microwave on 30-second intervals until the soap base is completely melted, stirring in between intervals.

2. Add the bentonite clay and stir until thoroughly mixed.

3. Quickly pour the mixture into a silicone mold and set aside.

4. Allow the soap to set for a few hours before popping them out of the mold.

Anti-Acne Goat's Milk Soap

This unscented moisturizing soap is great for dry and sensitive skin.

Ingredients

- 7 oz. coconut oil
- 5 oz. shea butter
- 14 oz. olive oil
- 1.76 oz. castor oil
- 3.5 oz. goat's milk, partially frozen
- 3.5 oz. water
- 3.8 oz. lye

Instructions

1. Place water in a heat-resistant container. Slowly add the lye and stir until it has totally dissolved. Set aside and allow the solution to cool to 100°F.

2. Add the partially frozen goat's milk. This should bring the solution's temperature down.

3. Immediately after adding the milk to the lye solution, place the coconut oil and shea butter in a pan over low heat. Once the solid oils have melted, remove the pan from heat and add the olive oil and castor oil. Allow the oils to cool to 90°F.

4. Once the oils have cooled down and the temperatures of the two mixtures are within 10° of each other, carefully pour the lye solution into the oil mix. Blend using a stick blender, alternating between manually stirring and pulsing. Bring the mixture to a medium trace.

5. Pour the soap mixture into the mold and cover it with a plastic wrap. Refrigerate for 24 hours.

6. This soap requires more time to harden and could break if cut too soon. So after taking it out of the fridge, leave it on your counter for 3 to 4 days. After that, you can remove it from the mold and slice into bars. Allow the soap to cure for 3 to 4 weeks before using.

Bamboo Charcoal Soap

Beauty products containing charcoal are quite popular because they gently exfoliate and get rid of dirt and oil in the pores without leaving residues behind. You can enjoy the many skin care benefits of bamboo charcoal powder with this soap, no matter what your skin type is.

Ingredients

- 9.6 oz. palm oil

- 8 oz. coconut oil

- 8 oz. olive oil

- 4.8 oz. palm kernel oil

- 1.6 oz. castor oil

- 12.1 oz. water

- 4.7 oz. lye

- 1 tbsp. bamboo charcoal powder

- 0.9 oz. peppermint essential oil

Instructions

1. Place the water in a heatproof container. Slowly add the lye and stir until it has completely dissolved. Set aside and allow the solution to cool to 90-100°F.

2. Place the coconut oil and palm oil in a pot over low heat. Once melted, add the olive oil, palm kernel oil, and castor oil. Remove from heat and allow the mixture to cool to 90-100°F.

3. Combine the bamboo charcoal powder with 2 tbsp. of the melted oil. Mix until fully dissolved. Set aside.

4. Once the two mixtures have reached the right temperature, carefully pour the lye solution into the oil mix. Blend using a stick blender. Alternate between pulsing and manually stirring until the mixture reaches a light trace. Be vigilant when blending since the palm kernel oil in the batter can speed up trace.

5. Stir in the essential oil and dissolved bamboo charcoal. Blend and bring the mixture to a medium trace.

6. Pour the soap batter into your prepared loaf mold. Insulate the soap by covering the mold with a piece of cardboard and a towel.

7. Remove the soap from the mold after at least 24 hours or once it has fully hardened. Cut it into bars and let them cure for 4 to 6 weeks.

Chamomile and Lavender Facial Soap

The extra jojoba oil and shea butter in this melt-and-pour soap recipe hydrates and nourishes dry skin. The chamomile essential oil and extract can help soothe irritation, making this facial soap ideal for those with sensitive skin.

Ingredients

- 24 oz. shea melt-and-pour soap base

- 0.5 oz. jojoba oil

- 0.5 oz. shea butter

- 0.19 oz. chamomile extract

- 0.04 oz. chamomile essential oil

- 0.08 oz. lavender essential oil

Instructions

1. Cut the soap base into small cubes and place them in a microwave-safe bowl. Melt the soap in the microwave using 30-second increments.

2. Melt the shea butter in a separate container using 10-second bursts. Once melted, add it to the soap.

3. Stir in all the other ingredients. Mix until they're fully dispersed.

4. Pour the soap mixture into your prepared mold. If necessary, lightly spray the top with isopropyl alcohol to get rid of bubbles.

5. Set the soap aside for at least 2 hours to cool and fully harden before removing them from the mold.

Charcoal Soap with Tea Tree Oil

This charcoal soap recipe is formulated for combination to oily skin and has the healing properties of tea tree oil. It also uses oils that are great for facial skin.

Ingredients

- 14.4 oz. olive oil

- 9 oz. coconut oil

- 9 oz. palm oil

- 1.8 oz. castor oil

- 1.8 oz. Tamanu oil

- 10.1 oz. distilled water

- 5.1 oz. lye

- 2 tbsp. activated charcoal

- 0.7 oz. tea tree essential oil

Instructions

1. Slowly add the lye to the water. Stir until the liquid is clear and the lye has totally dissolved. Set aside and allow the solution to cool to 100-120°F.

2. Heat up all the oils, except for tea tree oil, until the mixture has fully melted. Remove from heat and allow to cool.

3. Once the temperatures of the two mixture are within 10° of each other, carefully pour the lye solution to the oil mix. Blend using a stick blender and bring the mixture to a light trace.

4. Add activated charcoal to the soap mixture. Stir in the essential oil with the stick blender and blend until completely mixed. Bring the mixture to a medium trace.

5. Pour soap mixture into the mold and tap it on your counter. Remove any bubbles and prevent soda ash from forming by lightly spraying the top with 99% isopropyl alcohol.

6. Insulate the soap for 24 hours by covering the mold with a sheet of wax paper and a towel. Leave it undisturbed for another 2 to 3 days and then check if it has hardened. This soap contains plenty of soft oil and may require up to a week to solidify. Once it's firm enough, remove the soap from the mold and let them cure for at least 4 weeks.

Charcoal Soap

Here's an easier version of the previous recipe using the melt-and-pour method.

Ingredients

- 1 lb. shea melt-and-pour soap base

- 2 tsp. activated charcoal

- 0.4 oz. tea tree essential oil

Instructions

1. Cut the soap base into small chunks and place them in a microwave-safe dish. Microwave the mixture in 30-second intervals until the soap base has fully melted, stirring in between.

2. Add the charcoal and mix until no clumps remain.

3. Add the lavender oil and mix until oil is fully incorporated.

4. Pour melted soap into the cavities of your mold. Allow soap to cool and harden for a few hours before popping them out of the mold.

Cucumber Soap

This palm-free soap recipe is great for acne-prone skin. It's also helpful for itchy and inflamed skin.

Ingredients

- 3 oz. unpeeled cucumber

- 12 oz. olive oil

- 8 oz. coconut oil

- 4 oz. rice bran oil

- 2 oz. avocado oil

- 2 oz. shea butter

- 6 oz. chilled water

- 3.83 oz. lye

- 0.15 oz. French green clay + 2 tbsp. water

Instructions

1. Mix cucumber with 2 ounces of chilled water in a food processor and puree. Transfer the fresh puree into a container and add enough water until the mixture weighs 9 ounces.

2. Slowly add lye to the mixture. Stir until lye is completely dissolved. Set aside and allow to cool to 100-110°F. This will take about 30 to 40 minutes.

3. Place the coconut oil and shea butter in a pot over low heat. Once they begin to melt, add the olive oil, rice bran oil, and avocado oil. Remove from heat when the solids have fully melted. Allow the oils to cool to 100-110°F.

4. Once the two mixtures are about the same temperature, add the lye/cucumber solution to the oils. Using a stick blender, bring the mixture to a light trace.

5. Stir in the clay and water mixture. If you want to add fragrance or essential oils, do so now.

6. Transfer the soap into your prepared mold and leave it in the freezer for 24 hours. Remove soap from the mold and slice into bars. Cure the soap bars for at least 4 weeks.

Facial Scrub for Men

Who says beauty soaps are only for women? This facial scrub for men with fruity fragrance cleanses deeply and nourishes the skin. It contains poppy seeds, which exfoliate the skin and unblock the pores.

Ingredients

- 6 oz. olive oil

- 6 oz. sunflower oil

- 5 oz. coconut oil

- 8 oz. distilled water

- 2.5 oz. lye

- 0.16 oz. (1 tsp.) grapefruit essential oil

- 0.16 oz. (1 tsp.) cinnamon leaf essential oil

- 0.16 oz. (1 tsp.) orange essential oil

- 2 tbsp. poppy seeds

Instructions

1. Place water in a glass or sturdy plastic jug. Slowly add the lye and stir until it has totally dissolved. Set aside and allow the solution to cool to 90-100°F.

2. Place the olive oil, coconut oil, and sunflower oil in a large pan. Put them over low heat. Once the solid oils have melted, remove from heat and allow to cool.

3. Once the temperatures of the two mixtures are at 90-100°F, carefully pour the lye solution to the oil mix. Blend using a stick blender and bring the mixture to a light trace.

4. Add the essential oils and poppy seeds to the soap mixture. Blend until completely mixed and bring the mixture to a medium trace.

5. Pour soap mixture into the cavities of your mold. Insulate the soap for 24 to 48 hours by covering the mold with a sheet of wax paper and a towel. Once it's firm enough, remove the soap from the mold and let them cure for at least 4 weeks.

Green Clay and Kelp Facial Soap

The green clay and kelp granules in this soap gently exfoliate and keep skin soft and smooth. They also give the soap a natural green color.

Ingredients

- 1 lb. detergent-free aloe and olive soap

- 0.4 oz. green zeolite clay

- 0.3 oz. kelp granules

- 0.3 oz. Litsea cubeba essential oil

Instructions

1. Cut the soap base into small cubes and place them in a microwave-safe bowl. Melt the soap in the microwave using 30-second intervals, stirring in between bursts.

2. Once the soap base has completely melted, add the zeolite clay and kelp granules. Mix until soap is evenly colored. Add the essential oil and stir to disperse.

3. Pour the soap mixture into your prepared mold. Lightly spray with alcohol to get rid of bubbles.

4. Set the soap aside for at least 2 hours to cool and harden. Remove soap from the mold after it has fully hardened.

Green Tea Soap with French Green Clay

The oils in this recipe include grapeseed, rice bran, and hazelnut, which are known to preserve the skin's natural moisture and slow down the formation of wrinkles.

Ingredients

- 5.25 oz. coconut oil

- 4.2 oz. palm oil

- 4.2 oz. grapeseed oil

- 3.15 oz. rice bran oil

- 3.15 oz. hazelnut oil

- 1.05 oz. shea butter

- 4.38 oz. brewed green tea

- 2.92 oz. lye

- 0.6 oz. green tea fragrance oil

- 0.1 oz. French green clay

Instructions

1. Before starting, place the green tea in an ice cube tray and put it in the freezer.

2. Transfer the frozen green tea cubes into a heatproof container. Slowly add the lye and mix. The heat from the dissolving lye will melt the green tea cubes. Set aside.

3. Place the coconut oil, palm oil, and shea butter in a pot over low heat. Once melted, add the grapeseed, rice bran, and hazelnut oils. Remove from heat and set aside.

4. Once the temperatures of the two mixtures reach 90-100°F, pour the lye solution into the oil mix. Blend using a stick blender, alternating between manually stirring and pulsing. Bring the mixture to a light trace.

5. Add the French green clay and mix until no clumps remain. Stir in the essential oil and bring the batter to a medium trace.

6. Pour the soap batter into the cavities of your mold and put it in the freezer. After 24 hours, remove the soap from the mold and allow them to cure for at least 4 weeks.

Luxurious Face Soap

If you have oily skin, this simple melt-and-pour soap recipe is perfect for you.

Ingredients

- 1 lb. white melt-and-pour soap base

- 0.5 oz. sunflower or avocado oil

- 0.16 oz. (1 tsp.) shea butter

- 0.17 oz. (1 tsp.) beeswax chips

Instructions

1. Place the oil, shea butter, and beeswax in a microwave-safe bowl. Heat until wax melts.

2. Cut the soap base into small chunks and place them in another microwave-safe bowl. Cover it with Saran Wrap and microwave in 30-second intervals, stirring the soap in between.

3. Once the soap base has completely melted, stir in the melted oil mixture. Mix until well combined.

4. Pour soap into the mold. If you see any bubbles, lightly spray them with isopropyl alcohol. Allow to soap to cool and harden for a couple of hours before popping them out of the mold.

Orange and Clove Soap

Infused with essential oils known for their antiseptic properties, this soap is a great supplement to the treatment of acne.

Ingredients

- 1 lb. goat's milk melt-and-pour soap base

- 0.08 oz. (½ tsp.) orange essential oil

- 0.03 oz. (15 drops) clove essential oil

- 2 tbsp. dried orange peel

- 2 tsp. ground clove

Instructions

1. Cut the soap base into small cubes and put them in a microwave-safe bowl. Melt in the microwave using 30-second intervals, stirring after each burst.

2. Once the soap base is completely melted, add the orange peel and ground clove and mix thoroughly.

3. Stir in the essential oil and mix to disperse.

4. Pour the mixture into the cavities of your prepared mold. Allow soap to completely cool and harden for a few hours before removing them from the mold.

Tea Tree and Rosemary Facial Soap

This facial soap is best for cleansing oily skin. It contains clay that absorbs excess oil and olive leaf powder that has antiseptic properties.

Ingredients

- 24 oz. white melt-and-pour soap base

- 0.08 0z. (1/2 tsp.) tea tree essential oil

- 0.08 oz. (½ tsp.) Rosemary essential oil

- 4 tsp. zeolite clay

- 2 tsp. olive leaf powder

Instructions

1. Cut the soap base into small cubes and place them in a microwave-safe bowl. Melt the soap in the microwave using 30-second increments, stirring after each interval.

2. Once soap base has completely melted, stir in the olive leaf powder and zeolite clay. Mix until they're fully dispersed and no chunks of powder remain. Add the essential oils and mix thoroughly.

3. Pour the soap mixture into your prepared mold. If necessary, lightly spray the top with isopropyl alcohol to get rid of bubbles.

4. Set the soap aside for at least 2 hours to cool and fully harden before removing them from the mold.

Recipes for Hair Care

Goat's Milk and Honey Soap

This natural shampoo bar doubles as a body soap. The beeswax in the recipe helps protect the hair, while the combination of goat's milk and honey has great benefits for the skin.

Ingredients

- 9 oz. coconut oil

- 9 oz. olive oil

- 5 oz. castor oil

- 3 oz. jojoba oil

- 2 oz. shea butter

- 2 oz. cocoa butter

- 1 oz. beeswax

- 10 oz. goat's milk, partially frozen

- 4 0z. lye

- 0.75 oz. raw honey

- 0.5 oz. essential oils

Instructions

1. Place all the oils (except for essential oils), butters, and beeswax in a large pot and melt under low heat. Remove from heat once all solids have completely melted. Set aside and allow to cool to 100-110°F.

2. With the partially frozen goat's milk in a stainless steel or plastic container, add a small amount of lye and stir until it dissolves. Once the solution cools down a bit, add more lye and stir. Repeat adding lye in small amounts, keeping the solution from exceeding 100°F.

3. Once the two mixtures are at about the same temperature, add the lye/milk solution to the melted oils. Mix with the stick blender on and off. Bring the mixture to a light trace.

4. Add the honey and essential oils. Mix until honey is thoroughly incorporated into the mixture and the batter is at a medium trace.

5. Transfer the soap mixture into your prepared mold and refrigerate for at least 24 hours to cool and harden. Remove soap from the mold and cure for 4 to 6 weeks.

Lavender and Peppermint Shampoo Bar

The scent of this shampoo and body bar is a fun combination of lavender and mint—relaxing and refreshing.

Ingredients

- 10.18 oz. coconut oil

- 5.09 oz. sunflower oil

- 3.82 oz. palm oil

- 2.55 oz. castor oil

- 2.55 oz. jojoba oil

- 2.55 oz. Argan oil

- 1.27 oz. cocoa butter

- 10.64 oz. water

- 0.25 oz. lavender essential oil

- 0.25 oz. peppermint essential oil

Instructions

1. Place water in a heatproof container. Slowly add the lye and stir until it has completely dissolved. Set aside and allow the solution to cool to 100-110°F.

2. Place the coconut oil, palm oil, and cocoa butter in a pot over low heat. Once melted, add the sunflower, castor, argan, and jojoba oils. Remove from heat and allow the mixture to cool to 100-110°F.

3. Once the two mixtures have cooled down to the right temperature, carefully pour the lye solution into the oil mix.

Blend using a stick blender. Alternate between pulsing and manually stirring until the mixture reaches a light trace.

4. Stir in the essential oils. Blend until they're fully dispersed and the batter has reached a medium trace.

5. Pour the soap batter into your prepared loaf mold. Cover the mold with a sheet of wax paper or cardboard and a towel to insulate the soap.

6. After 24 hours or when the soap has completely hardened, release it from the mold. Slice soap into bars and allow to cure for at least 4 weeks.

Rosemary and Mint Shampoo Bar

Infused with rosemary and mint, this shampoo bar will leave you smelling great. It doubles as a body soap, too.

Ingredient

- 10 oz. olive oil

- 8 oz. coconut oil

- 4 oz. castor oil

- 4 oz. sunflower oil

- 2 oz. jojoba oil

- 10 oz. distilled water

- 3.82 oz. lye

- 0.5 oz. peppermint essential oil

- 0.16 oz. Rosemary essential oil

Instructions

1. Place the water in a heatproof container. Slowly add the lye and stir until it has completely dissolved. Set aside and allow the solution to cool to around 100°F.

2. Place the coconut oil in a pot over low heat. Once melted, remove the pot from heat and add the olive, castor, sunflower, and jojoba oils. Allow the mixture to cool to around 100°F.

3. Once the two mixtures have reached the right temperature, carefully pour the lye solution into the oil mix. Blend using a stick blender. Alternate between pulsing and manually stirring until the mixture reaches a light trace.

4. Stir in the essential oils. Blend until they're fully dispersed and the batter has reached a medium trace.

5. Pour the soap batter into your prepared mold. Cover the mold with a sheet of wax paper or cardboard. Insulate the soap for at least 24 hours by covering it with a towel.

6. Remove soap from the mold and slice it into bars. Cure the soap bars for 4 to 6 weeks.

Conditioner Bar

Making your own solid conditioner is quite easy. The hardest part is actually gathering the required ingredients. Once you have them, all you need to do is melt and wait.

Ingredients

- 1.06 oz. cocoa butter

- 1.06 oz. incroquat

- 0.71 oz. cetyl alcohol

- 0.71 oz. grapeseed oil

- 0.14 oz. beeswax

- 0.13 oz. fragrance oil

- 0.19 oz. hydrolyzed keratin

Instructions

1. Place all the ingredients in a small saucepan and slowly melt them over low heat, stirring regularly. Don't worry if you smell something unpleasant while the ingredients are melting. It's normal and it will go away in no time.

2. Pour the melted ingredients into the mold. Set it aside for a few hours to cool down. You can also place it in the fridge.

3. Remove the conditioner from the mold. Let it rest for at least 24 hours before using.

Chapter 4: Colorful and Beautiful Soap Recipes

Colorful Soap Recipes

Blue Crystal Soap

Crystal soaps are quite easy to make and are ideal for beginners. This soap is scented with Alpine Frost, which perfectly complements its cool blue color.

Ingredients

- 2 lbs. clear melt-and-pour soap base

- 0.7 oz. Alpine Frost fragrance oil

- 1/8 tsp. fine silver glitters

- blue soap colorant

Instructions

1. Cut the soap base into small cubes and place them in a microwave-safe bowl. Melt the soap in the microwave in 30-second bursts, stirring in between each burst.

2. Once the soap base has completely melted, stir in the fragrance oil. Add the colorant a few drops at a time, mixing thoroughly until your desired shade of blue is achieved.

3. Pour the soap into a silicone mold with 12 cavities. If there are bubbles forming on your soap, lightly spray it with isopropyl alcohol. Allow soap to cool and harden for at least 2 hours.

4. Remove soap bars from the mold and cut them into gem shapes using a non-serrated knife.

5. Gather the scraps and melt them in the microwave in 15-second intervals. Pour melted soap in the mold, and cut the bars into gem shapes once they have completely hardened.

Cactus Soap

Making this glittery cactus soap is just as easy as making any layered melt-and-pour soap. The only other thing you need is a 6-cavity cactus mold.

Ingredients

- 19 oz. white melt-and-pour soap base

- 6 oz. clear melt-and-pour soap base

- 0.6 oz. fragrance oil

- green and blue soap colorant

- biodegradable glitters

Instructions

1. Cut the white soap base into small cubes. Take 3 oz. of the cubes and melt them in the microwave. Once melted, stir in 0.1 oz. of fragrance oil and some green soap colorant and mix thoroughly. Add the colorant little by little until your desired shade of green is achieved.

2. Pour the soap mixture into the cactus mold. Lightly spray with alcohol if there are bubbles. Set aside.

3. Melt the remaining white soap base in the microwave using 30-second bursts. Once melted, stir in 0.45 oz. of fragrance oil. Add the blue colorant and mix until your desired shade of blue is achieved.

4. Pour the soap mixture evenly into a 6-cavity rectangular mold. If there are bubbles forming on your soap, lightly spray it with alcohol. Set aside.

5. Once the cactus soaps have hardened, remove them from the mold. Spray the blue soap with alcohol and place a cactus soap on top of each. Set aside.

6. Melt the clear soap base in the microwave. Once melted, add some glitters and the remaining fragrance oil. Mix thoroughly to disperse.

7. Spray the soaps in the mold with alcohol and pour in the melted soap evenly. Spray a little more alcohol to get rid of any bubbles. Set aside to cool and harden before removing the soap bars from the mold.

Potted Succulent Soap

To shape this melt-and-pour soap into potted succulents, you'll need a succulent mold and four 3-oz. disposable cups.

Ingredients

- 16 oz. white melt-and-pour soap base

- 0.4 oz. essential oil

- green and gray soap colorant

Instructions

1. Cut the soap base into small cubes. Take 4 oz. of the cubes and melt them in the microwave. Once melted, add 0.2 oz. of essential oil. Add some green colorant and mix to fully incorporate.

2. Pour the soap mixture into a 4-cavity succulent mold. If there are bubbles, lightly spray the soap with alcohol. Set aside to cool and harden.

3. To make the pots, melt 10 oz. of the soap base in the microwave. Once melted, add the remaining essential oil. Stir in some gray colorant until you're satisfied with the color.

4. Divide the soap mixture evenly between the 4 cups. Spray with alcohol to get rid of bubbles. Set aside.

5. Cut some of the remaining soap bases into smaller pieces to resemble pebbles. Once the succulent soaps have hardened, melt the remaining soap base. Place some soap pebbles on top of each pot. Spray with alcohol and pour into each pot to hold the pebbles in place.

6. Remove the succulents from the mold and press one on top of each pot. Remove the disposable cup after the soap has completely hardened.

Recycled Soap

If you have lots of soap scraps—whether homemade or store-bought—you can give them a new life using this recipe.

Ingredients

- 9.6 oz. lard
- 8 oz. coconut oil
- 4.8 0z. shea butter
- 4.8 oz. safflower oil
- 3.2 oz. rice bran oil
- 1.6 oz. castor oil
- 12.16 oz. water
- 4.49 oz. lye
- 1 lb. soap scraps (of various colors)
- 1.5 oz. fragrance oil
- 0.6 oz. white kaolin clay

Instructions

1. Chop the soap scraps into tiny bits with a blender. Set aside.

2. Place the water in a heatproof container. Slowly add the lye and stir until it has completely dissolved. Set aside and allow the solution to cool to 90-100°F.

3. Place the lard, coconut oil, and shea butter in a pot over low heat. Once melted, add the safflower, rice bran, and castor oils.

Remove the pot from heat and allow the mixture to cool to 90-100°F.

4. Once the two mixtures have reached the right temperature, carefully pour the lye solution into the oil mix. Blend using a stick blender. Alternate between pulsing and manually stirring until the mixture reaches a light trace.

5. Stir in the kaolin clay and fragrance oil. Continue blending until the mixture reaches a medium trace. Add the soap bits and mix to disperse.

6. Pour or spoon the soap batter into your prepared loaf mold. Insulate soap by covering the mold with a piece of cardboard and a towel.

7. After at least 24 hours, remove soap from the mold. Cut it into bars and let them cure for at least 4 weeks.

Rosemary and Lavender Hand Soap

This pretty bar of soap cleans dirty hands without stripping the skin's natural moisture. It also contains poppy seeds, which work as a light exfoliant and give the soap a lovely speckled look.

Ingredients

- 7.9 oz. olive oil

- 3.9 oz. coconut oil

- 3.2 oz. sunflower oil

- 0.77 oz. cocoa butter

- 0.23 oz. shea butter

- 5.6 oz. water

- 2.23 oz. lye

- 0.3 oz. lavender essential oil

- 0.15 oz. Rosemary essential oil

- 1.5 tsp. poppy seeds

- 1/8 tsp. ultramarine violet colorant

Instructions

1. In a ramekin or small container, mix the colorant with 1 tsp. olive oil. Set aside.

2. Place the water in a heatproof container. Slowly add the lye and stir until it has completely dissolved. Set aside and allow the solution to cool to around 120°F.

3. Place the coconut oil, cocoa butter, and shea butter in a pot over low heat. Once melted, remove the pot from heat and add the olive oil and sunflower oil. Allow the mixture to cool to around 120°F.

4. Once the two mixtures have reached the right temperature, carefully pour the lye solution to the oil mix. Blend using a stick blender. Alternate between pulsing and manually stirring until the mixture reaches a light trace.

5. Stir in the essential oils, poppy seeds, and clay-oil mix. Blend until the color has fully dispersed and the batter has reached a medium trace.

6. Pour the soap batter into your prepared mold. Cover the mold with a sheet of wax paper or cardboard and insulate the soap for at least 24 hours by covering it with a towel.

7. Remove soap from the mold and slice it into bars. Let them cure for 4 to 6 weeks before use.

Swirled Soap Recipes

Champagne and Orange Faux-Swirl Soap

Ingredients

- 10.24 oz. coconut oil

- 12.8 oz. olive oil

- 5.12 oz. cocoa butter

- 3.84 oz. castor oil

- 4.57 oz. lye

- 12.16 oz. distilled water

- 0.3 oz. champagne fragrance

- 0.2 oz. orange essential oil

- pink liquid colorant

Instructions

1. Place the water in a heat-resistant container and slowly add the lye. Stir until the lye has totally dissolved. Set aside and allow the solution to cool to around 100-110°F.

2. Place the coconut oil and cocoa butter in a pot over low heat. Once melted, add the olive oil and castor oil. Remove from heat and allow the mixture to cool to around 100-110°F.

3. Once the two mixtures reach the right temperature, carefully pour the lye solution into the oil mix. Blend using a stick blender, alternating between manually stirring and pulsing. Bring the mixture to a light trace and then transfer about 1/3 of the batter into another container.

4. Add a few drops of colorant to the main container. Stir just to disperse the color. Avoid overmixing.

5. Add the same amount (or more) of colorant to the other container and mix. You want this batter to be much darker than the other.

6. Add the fragrance and essential oil to the main container. Stir manually, keeping the batter at light trace.

7. Pour the darker soap into the main container, from about 10 inches above. This will give the soap a swirled look. Immediately pour the batter into your prepared loaf mold.

8. Cover the mold and insulate it with a towel. After about 24 hours, remove the soap from the mold and cut into bars. Cure the bars for 4 to 6 weeks.

Cool Blue Soap

Ingredients

- 8.8 oz. coconut oil

- 8.8 oz. palm oil

- 8.8 oz. olive oil

- 4.2 oz. rice bran oil

- 3.5 oz. avocado oil

- 1 oz. castor oil

- 10.4 oz. distilled water

- 4.9 oz. lye

- 1.25 oz. fragrance oil

- 3 tbsp. sunflower oil

- 1 tsp. titanium dioxide

- 1 tsp. ultramarine blue soap colorant

- 1 tsp. neon blue soap colorant

Instructions

1. In three separate ramekins or glasses, combine the titanium dioxide and soap colorants with 1 tbsp. of sunflower oil each. Mix thoroughly to disperse and get rid of clumps. Set aside.

2. Place the water in a heatproof container and slowly add the lye. Stir until the lye has totally dissolved. Set aside and allow the solution to cool to 100-110°F.

3. Place all the oils (except for fragrance oil) in a large pot over low heat. Once the solid oils have fully melted, remove the pot from heat. Allow the oil mix to cool to 100-110°F.

4. Once the two mixtures have reached the right temperature, carefully pour the lye solution into the oil mix. Blend using a stick blender. Alternate between manually mixing and pulsing. Bring the mixture to a light trace.

5. Split the batter into 4 equal parts. Transfer ¼ into another container and whisk in 1.5 tsp. of dispersed neon blue colorant. Place another ¼ in a separate container and whisk in 2 tsp. of ultramarine blue colorant. Mix all the dispersed titanium dioxide with the remaining batter.

6. Add fragrance oil to each container and whisk to disperse the fragrance.

7. Pour some of the white batters into a loaf mold to cover the bottom. Next, alternate pouring or spooning the three colors into the mold. Add small amounts at varying heights each time so your soap won't form layers.

8. Swirl the batter using a thin bamboo stick or chopstick. For a more complex design, use a hanger swirl tool. Using a spoon, smooth the top of the soap.

9. Place a sheet of wax paper or cardboard on top of the mold and cover it with a towel to insulate. Remove the cover after 24 hours, but keep the soap in the mold for 1 or 2 more days.

10. Remove soap from the mold and cut it into bars. Cure the bars of soap for 4 to 6 weeks.

Honey Soap

Ingredients

- 7.58 oz. olive oil

- 1.76 oz. castor oil

- 5.29 oz. coconut oil

- 2.65 oz. shea butter

- 0.35 oz. beeswax

- 4.3 oz. water

- 2.45 oz. lye

- 0.37 oz. honey

- ½ tsp. powdered gold mica

Instructions

1. Combine the gold mica and 1 tbsp. olive oil in a ramekin or a small container. Mix thoroughly and set aside.

2. Place the water in a heat-resistant container and slowly add the lye. Stir until the lye has totally dissolved. Set aside and allow the solution to cool to around 110°F.

3. Place the coconut oil, shea butter, and beeswax in a pot or large pan over low heat. Remove from heat when once solid oils have melted and add the olive oil and castor oil. Allow the mixture to cool to around 110°F.

4. Once the temperatures of the two mixtures are within 10° of each other, carefully pour the lye solution into the oil mix. Blend using a stick blender, alternating between manually stirring and pulsing. Bring the mixture to a light trace and then stir in the honey until it's completely dispersed.

5. Place about 1/3 of the batter into another container. Add the colorant and stir until it's fully incorporated.

6. Pour the soap mixture into the mold, alternating between the uncolored and gold batter. Using a thin bamboo stick or chopstick, lightly swirl the batter.

7. Cover the mold with a sheet of wax paper or cardboard and insulate it with a towel. After at least 24 hours, remove the soap from the mold. If you're using a loaf mold, cut your soap into bars. Cure the soap bars for 4 to 6 weeks.

Raspberry Swirled Soap

This recipe also calls for the addition of titanium dioxide to make the colors pop, although it's optional and your soap will still be perfectly fine without it.

Ingredients

- 11.8 oz. palm oil

- 10.6 oz. coconut oil

- 9.6 oz. olive oil

- 12.16 oz. water

- 4.67 oz. lye

- 0.9 oz. raspberry fragrance oil

- 1 tsp. titanium dioxide

- 1 tsp. red mica

Instructions

1. Mix 1 tbsp. of olive oil with the red mica in a small glass or ramekin. In another glass, mix 1 tbsp. of olive oil with titanium dioxide (but check the packaging first to make sure what type of liquid it requires). Stir both mixtures well until diluted and there are no more lumps. Set the glasses aside.

2. Place the vegetable fat and coconut oil in a pan and melt over the stove on low heat. Add the olive oil once the solids have melted. Remove from heat.

3. Pour the water into a glass container and slowly add the lye. Stir gently until the lye has completely dissolved. Set aside to cool.

4. When the two mixtures are at roughly the same temperature (120-140°F), pour the lye solution into the melted oil. Blend the mixture with a stick blender and bring it to a light trace. Once it reaches the desired consistency, scoop out 3 spoonfuls of the soap mixture into a separate container.

5. Add fragrance oil to the pan of soap mixture and mix. Add the titanium dioxide mixture and stir until it's fully incorporated.

6. Add the red colorant mixture to the soap mixture in a separate container. Stir until fully mixed.

7. Pour the soap batter halfway up the loaf mold. Dribble a spoonful of the colored soap on the batter. Quickly stir the mixture a few times with a thin bamboo stick or chopstick.

8. Add the remaining soap batter and spoon the rest of the colored soap. Stir the mixture a few times to achieve the marbled effect.

9. To insulate, cover the top of the mold with cardboard and place a towel over it. Leave the soap undisturbed for 24 to 48 hours.

10. Once the soap has hardened, remove it from the mold and slice it into rectangles. Leave the soap bars to cure for 4 to 6 weeks.

Shea and Cocoa Butter Soap

Ingredients:

- 5.4 oz. shea butter
- 5.8 oz. cocoa butter
- 15.6 oz. coconut oil
- 11.2 oz. olive oil
- 2.2 oz. castor oil
- 4.5 oz. lard
- 12.6 oz. water
- 6.3 oz. lye
- 2 oz. fragrance oil blend
- ½ Tsp. gold mica
- ½ Tsp. brown mica

Instructions

1. Place the cocoa butter into a bowl and microwave it for 3 minutes or until its partially melted. Add the shea butter. When it has partially melted, add the coconut and lard one at a time, and heat further. Add the olive and castor oils once the solid oils have completely melted. Remove from the oven and allow to cool.

2. While the oils are in the microwave, place the colorants into separate ramekins with 1 tbsp. of oil. Mix well.

3. Prepare the lye solution by adding lye to the water in a jar and mixing it using a non-metal utensil. Set it aside to cool.

4. Before adding the lye solution to your oils, make sure that they're within 10° of each other. Mix them until you reach a trace. Add the fragrance oil blend and stir a bit.

5. Combine one of the colorants with one cup of soap and the other one with another cup. Mix well and then swirl them back into the bowl. You can use a stick blender that's turned off to swirl the colors in.

6. Transfer the soap into your mold. After at least 24 hours, pop the bars out of the mold and let them cure for 4 to 6 weeks.

Layered Soap Recipes

Peaches and Cream Soap

Making this soap with two layers shouldn't be more difficult than the other melt-and-pour soap recipes. You only have to be careful about when to pour the next layer.

Ingredients

- 1 lb. goat's milk melt-and-pour soap base

- 0.16 oz. (1 tsp.) peach fragrance oil

- ¼ tsp. peach colorant

Instructions

1. Cut the soap base into small cubes and place half of the cubes in a microwave-safe bowl. Place the bowl in the microwave and melt the soap in 30-second intervals, stirring in between.

2. Once the soap base has completely melted, stir in the peach colorant and ½ tsp. fragrance oil. Mix until the color has been fully incorporated.

3. Pour soap into your prepared mold. Spritz some alcohol on the surface if there are bubbles forming on your soap. Allow the soap to cool and partially harden (about 30 minutes).

4. Once the soap in the mold is firm enough, melt the remaining soap base and then stir in the remaining fragrance oil.

5. Pour soap into the mold and spritz some alcohol to get rid of bubbles, if needed.

6. Set the soap aside for at least 2 hours to cool and harden. When the soap has fully hardened, remove it from the mold and slice into bars.

Chamomile Soap

Here's another 2-layered soap recipe that's perfect for your first ever layered soap.

Ingredients

- 1 lb. white melt-and-pour soap base

- 5 oz. clear melt-and-pour soap base

- 0.5 oz. (3 tsp.) chamomile fragrance oil

- dried chamomile herb

Instruction

1. Place some dried chamomile herb into the cavities of your mold. Set aside.

2. Cut the clear soap base into small cubes and place them in a microwave-safe bowl. Melt the soap in the microwave using 20-second intervals, stirring in between each burst.

3. Pour melted soap into each cavity to cover the herbs. If you see bubbles, lightly spray the soap with isopropyl alcohol. Set aside to cool and partially harden.

4. Cut the white soap base into small cubes and place them in a microwave-safe bowl. Melt the soap using 30-second intervals, stirring in between each burst.

5. Stir in the fragrance oil. Once the temperature of the melted soap reaches 125°F or less, pour it into each cavity of the mold. If there are bubbles, spray the bars of soap with isopropyl alcohol.

6. Sct the soap aside for at least 2 hours to cool and completely harden before removing them from the mold.

Cotton Candy Soap

Ingredients

- 2 lbs. white melt-and-pour soap base

- 0.5 oz. (2 tsp.) cotton candy fragrance oil

- pink, blue, and purple liquid soap colorant

Instructions

1. Divide the fragrance oil into 3 portions. Set aside.

2. Chop the soap base into small cubes. Melt 1/3 of the soap in the microwave using 30-second intervals, stirring in between.

3. Once melted, add purple colorant a few drops at a time and stir until a medium shade of purple is achieved. Stir in one portion of fragrance oil.

4. Pour the soap mixture into your prepared loaf mold. Lightly spray the top of the soap with isopropyl alcohol. Set aside.

5. When the first layer has partially hardened (about 15 minutes), melt another 1/3 of the soap. Add pink colorant and one portion of fragrance oil.

6. Lightly spray the first layer with alcohol and pour in the pink soap. Spray the top of the second layer with alcohol and set aside.

7. Do the same for the remaining soap and fragrance oil, adding the blue colorant. Spray the soap in the mold with alcohol and make sure it's firm enough before adding this final layer.

8. Spray the soap with alcohol to get rid of bubbles and set aside for a couple of hours to completely cool and harden. Release soap from the mold and slice into bars.

Indigo Ombre Soap

This 3-layered soap is naturally colored using indigo. Natural indigo is extracted from various types of plants and is known for its healing and antiseptic properties.

Ingredients

- 2 lbs. white melt-and-pour soap base

- 0.4 oz. (2.5 tsp.) lavender essential oil

- 0.4 oz. (2.5 tsp.) peppermint essential oil

- indigo powder

Instructions

1. Divide the essential oils into 3 portions. Set aside.

2. Chop the soap base into small chunks. Take 1/3 of the soap and melt it in the microwave. Stir soap after every 30 seconds.

3. Once melted, stir in 1/3 of the essential oils. Sprinkle a small amount of indigo powder and mix to fully incorporate. Add more indigo powder until you're satisfied with the color.

4. Pour the soap mixture into your prepared loaf mold. Lightly spray the top of the soap with isopropyl alcohol. Set aside.

5. When the first layer has partially hardened (about 15 minutes), melt another 1/3 of the soap and then stir in the essential oils. Add half of the amount of indigo you used for the first layer to make a lighter shade. Mix until the color is fully dispersed.

6. Lightly spray the first layer with alcohol and pour the melted soap. Spray the top of the second layer with alcohol and set aside.

7. Do the same for the remaining soap and essential oils. Add a tiny bit of indigo just to give the soap a hint of color. Make sure that the soap in the mold is firm enough before adding this final layer.

8. Allow the soap to completely harden before releasing it from the mold and slicing into bars.

Layered Gardener's Soap

Ingredients

- 1 lb. cocoa butter melt-and-pour soap base

- 0.5 oz. (1.5 tsp.) rosemary mint fragrance oil

- 1 tbsp. coffee grounds

- 1 tbsp. ground loofah

- 1 tbsp. ground pumice

- lime green liquid colorant

Instructions

1. Cut the soap base into small cubes. Melt 1/3 of the soap in the microwave, using 30-second burst, stirring soap in between.

2. Once melted, add the coffee grounds and ½ tsp. of fragrance oil. Mix thoroughly.

3. Pour the soap mixture into your prepared loaf mold. Lightly spray the top of the soap with isopropyl alcohol. Set aside.

4. When the first layer has partially hardened, melt another 1/3 of the soap. Add the loofah and ½ tsp. of fragrance oil.

5. Lightly spray the first layer with alcohol and pour the melted soap. Spray the top of the second layer with alcohol and set aside.

6. Melt the remaining soap. Add about 10 drops of colorant and mix until color is evenly dispersed. Feel free to use less or more colorant to achieve your desired shade of green. Stir in ½ tsp. of essential oil. Add the ground pumice and slowly stir until the soap is thick enough to keep them suspended.

7. Check if the soap in the mold is firm enough and then spray it with alcohol. Pour soap into the mold.

8. Allow soap to completely harden before releasing it from the mold and slicing into bars.

Mint Chocolate Soap

Ingredients

- 24 oz. clear melt-and-pour soap base

- 8 oz. white melt-and-pour soap base

- 0.2 oz. (1 tsp.) dark chocolate fragrance oil

- 0.08 oz. (½ tsp.) mint fragrance oil

- brown oxide color block

- chrome green color block

Instructions

1. Cut the clear soap base into small cubes and place them in a microwave-safe bowl. Melt the soap in the microwave using 30-second intervals, stirring in between each burst.

2. Add a few pieces of the brown colorant and mix to incorporate the color. Add some more colorant if you prefer a darker shade.

3. Add the chocolate fragrance oil and mix to disperse. Pour half of the soap into a loaf or tray mold. Lightly spray with alcohol to get rid of bubbles. Set aside to cool and partially harden.

4. Cut the clear soap base into small cubes and place them in a microwave-safe bowl. Melt the soap at 15-second intervals, stirring in between each burst.

5. Add some green colorant and mix until a light green color is achieved. Stir in the mint fragrance oil and mix thoroughly.

6. Once the temperature of the melted soap reaches 125°F or lower, pour it on top of the brown layer. Lightly spray with alcohol to get rid of bubbles. Set aside to cool and partially harden.

7. Re-melt the remaining brown soap and then pour it over the green layer. Make sure that the temperature is no more than 125°F before pouring. Spray the top with alcohol.

8. Set the soap aside for at least 2 hours to cool and completely harden. Remove it from the mold and cut into bars.

Neapolitan Ice Cream Soap

Ingredients

- 2 lbs. white melt-and-pour soap base

- 0.25 oz. (1.5 tsp.) vanilla fragrance oil

- 0.25 oz. (1.5 tsp.) chocolate fragrance oil

- 0.25 oz. (1.5 tsp.) strawberry fragrance oil

- brown and red soap colorant

Instructions

1. Chop the soap base into small cubes. Take 1/3 of the soap and melt it in the microwave, stirring after every 30 seconds.

2. Once melted, add a few drops of the red colorant and stir. Add colorant little by little until the soap turns strawberry pink. Stir in the strawberry fragrance oil and mix to disperse.

3. Pour the soap mixture into your prepared loaf mold. Spray the top with alcohol to get rid of bubbles. Set aside.

4. When the pink layer has partially hardened (about 15 minutes), melt another 1/3 of the soap and then stir in the vanilla essential oil.

5. Spray the first layer with alcohol and pour the melted soap. Spray the top of the second layer with alcohol and set aside.

6. Melt the remaining soap and add brown colorant a few drops at a time until a chocolate ice cream shade is achieved. Stir in the chocolate fragrance oil. Spray the soap in the mold with alcohol and make sure it's firm enough before adding this final layer.

7. Spray the soap with alcohol to get rid of bubbles. After it has completely hardened, release it from the mold and slice into bars.

Orange and Cranberry Soap

Ingredients

- 20 oz. white melt-and-pour soap base
- 0.35 oz. orange fragrance oil
- 0.2 oz. cranberry fragrance oil
- 0.05 oz. peppermint essential oil
- ¼ tsp. walnut shell powder
- red and yellow liquid soap colorant

Instructions

1. Chop the soap base into small chunks. Take 4 oz. of the soap and melt it in the microwave in 15-second bursts.

2. Once melted, stir in the walnut powder and peppermint essential oil. Mix thoroughly.

3. Divide the soap evenly between the cavities of your prepared mold. Lightly spray with alcohol to get rid of bubbles. Allow soap to partially harden.

4. Once the first layer is firm enough, melt 6 oz. of the soap base. Once melted, stir in the cranberry essential oil. Add 4 drops of red colorant and stir until color is evenly dispersed.

5. Spray the first layer with alcohol and divide the red soap evenly between each cavity. Set aside to partially harden.

6. For the third layer, melt 4 oz. of the soap base. Add 4 drops of red colorant and stir until the color is evenly dispersed.

7. Spray the second layer with alcohol and divide the soap evenly between each cavity. Before pouring, make sure that the second layer is firm enough.

8. Prepare the final layer when the third layer is almost ready. Melt the remaining soap base. Once melted, stir in the orange fragrance oil. Add 20 drops of yellow colorant and 3 drops of red colorant. Mix thoroughly.

9. Spray the soap in the mold with alcohol. Divide the orange soap evenly between each cavity. Spray the top again with alcohol to get rid of bubbles. Set aside to cool and harden before removing them from the mold.

Shea Gardener's Soap with Diagonal Layer

Ingredients

- 8 oz. shea melt-and-pour soap base
- 8 oz. clear melt-and-pour soap base
- 0.16 oz. (1 tsp.) fragrance oil
- 1 tbsp. ground walnut shell
- 1 tbsp. ground pumice
- violet liquid colorant

Instruction

1. Prop a small silicone loaf mold between 2 heavy objects, such as melt-and-pour blocks. Make sure the mold is level. This setup will make a diagonal layer.

2. Cut the clear soap base into small cubes and microwave until the soap base is completely melted, stirring every 30 seconds.

3. Add the ground pumice and walnut shell. Mix thoroughly, making sure that no clumps remain.

4. Add a generous amount of colorant and mix to achieve a rich violet color. Next, stir in ½ tsp. of fragrance oil.

5. Once the mixture is thick enough to keep the ground pumice and walnut shell suspended, pour it into the mold. Spray with alcohol to get rid of bubbles.

6. Melt the shea soap base in the microwave. Add the fragrance oil and stir thoroughly.

7. Once the first layer is firm enough, lay the mold flat and carefully pour the melted soap into the mold. Spray soap with alcohol.

8. Allow the soap to completely cool and harden before releasing it from the mold and slicing into bars.

Star-Studded Kid's Soap

Ingredients

- 1 lb. clear melt-and-pour soap base

- pink and blue soap colorant

- yellow star cupcake sprinkles

- edible star glitters

Instructions

1. Chop the soap base into small chunks. Place about a third of the chunks in a microwave-safe dish. Place the bowl in the microwave and melt the soap base in 30-second increments, stirring after each interval.

2. Once the soap base has fully melted, pour it into a mold with 4 rectangular cavities. Drop the star sprinkles and glitter. Lightly spray with alcohol. Allow soap to cool and slightly harden.

3. When the first layer is firm enough, melt about a third of the remaining soap. Once melted, add a drop of the blue colorant and stir thoroughly. Add more colorant until you're satisfied with the color.

4. Place a book under the mold so it's slightly tilted. Spoon in the blue soap on one side of each soap bar and lightly spray with alcohol. Allow the soap to cool with the mold still tilted.

5. When the blue soap is firm enough, do the same for the pink color using half of the remaining soap base. But this time, lay the mold flat before spooning in the melted pink soap. Lightly spray with alcohol and allow the soap to partially harden.

6. When the pink soap is firm enough, melt the remaining soap base and pour it into the mold and set aside. Remove bars from the soap after a couple of hours.

Turmeric Ombre Soap

This layered soap featuring 3 shades of orange is naturally colored using turmeric.

Ingredients

- 16.2 oz. coconut oil

- 13.5 oz. palm oil

- 10.8 oz. + 3 tbsp. sunflower oil

- 7 oz. olive oil

- 2.7 oz. shea butter

- 2.2 oz. cocoa butter

- 1.6 oz. castor oil

- 16 oz. distilled water

- 7.7 oz. lye

- 3 tsp. turmeric powder

Instructions

1. Combine turmeric powder and the 3 tbsp. of sunflower oil in a ramekin or glass. Mix to disperse and get rid of clumps. Set aside.

2. Place the distilled water in a heat-resistant container. Slowly add the lye to the water and stir until it has totally dissolved. Set aside and allow the solution to cool to 100-110°F.

3. Place all the oils in a large pot over low heat. Once the solid oils have fully melted, remove the pot from heat. Allow the oil mix to cool to 100-110°F.

4. Once the two mixtures have reached the right temperature, carefully pour the lye solution to the oil mix. Blend using a stick blender, alternating between manually mixing and pulsing. Bring the mixture to a light trace.

5. Split the batter equally into four containers. Whisk 4 tsp. of dispersed turmeric into one container. Using a stick blender, bring the mixture to a medium trace and pour the batter into a large (about 5 lbs.) loaf mold.

6. Whisk 1.5 tsp. of dispersed turmeric into another container. Bring the mixture to a medium trace using a stick blender and pour it over the first layer of soap.

7. Whisk the remaining soap mixture so they don't get too thick.

8. Whisk ¼ tsp. of dispersed turmeric into the third container. Blend until the color is fully incorporated and bring to medium trace if the batter hasn't thickened that much yet. Pour or spoon the batter into the mold.

9. If necessary, stick blend the last container to thicken. Pour or spoon the batter into the mold. Smooth the top using a spoon.

10. Place a sheet of wax paper or cardboard on top of the mold and cover it with a towel to insulate. Remove the cover after 24 hours but keep the soap in the mold for 2 more days.

11. Remove soap from the mold and cut it into bars. Allow the bars of soap to cure for 4 to 6 weeks.

Vanilla Mint Soap

This soap features a minty glycerin layer sandwiched between creamy vanilla-scented soap.

Ingredients

- 10 oz. white melt-and-pour soap base

- 7 oz. glycerin melt-and-pour soap base

- 0.08 oz. (½ tsp.) vanilla essential oil

- 0.04 oz. (¼ tsp.) peppermint essential oil

- green soap colorant

Instructions

1. Cut the white soap base into small cubes and place 5 oz. in a microwave-safe bowl. Melt the soap in the microwave in 30-second intervals, stirring in between.

2. Once soap base has completely melted, add 20 drops of vanilla essential oil. Mix thoroughly to disperse the oil.

3. Pour the soap into a cube silicone mold. If there are bubbles forming on your soap, lightly spray it with alcohol.

4. After about 20 minutes or when the first layer is firm enough, chop the glycerin and melt the soap in the microwave.

5. Once the soap base has completely melted, add the peppermint essential oil and 1 or 2 drops of colorant, depending on what shade of green you want. Mix thoroughly and then pour into the mold.

6. When the green layer is firm enough, melt the remaining white soap base. Stir in 20 drops of vanilla essential oil and pour the soap into the mold.

7. Set the soap aside for at least 2 hours to cool and harden. When the soap has fully hardened, remove it from the mold and slice into bars.

Watermelon Soap

Ingredients

- 1 lb. goat's milk melt-and-pour soap base

- 3 lbs. clear melt-and-pour soap base

- 0.08 oz. (½ tsp.) watermelon fragrance oil

- 1 tbsp. poppy seeds

- green and red soap colorant

Instructions

1. Cut the goat's milk soap base into small chunks and place ½ pound in a microwave-safe container. Melt the soap in 30-second bursts, stirring after each interval.

2. Once the soap has fully melted, stir in 10 drops of fragrance oil. Add the green colorant a few drops at a time, mixing thoroughly to incorporate the color, until your desired shade of green is achieved.

3. Pour ¾ of the melted soap into the prepared loaf mold. Lightly spray the top with alcohol if you see any bubbles. Allow soap to cool and partially harden.

4. After 15 to 20 minutes, add a ¼ pound of soap base chunks to the remaining green soap. Melt in the microwave and stir thoroughly. The color will become light green.

5. Check to see if the green layer is already firm enough and then add the melted soap. Allow soap to cool and partially harden.

6. After 15 to 20 minutes, melt another ¼ pound of soap base chunks in the microwave. Stir in 5 drops of fragrance oil.

7. Pour soap into the mold after making sure that the light green layer is firm enough. Allow soap to cool and partially harden.

8. After 15 minutes, cut the clear soap base into small chunks and melt in the microwave. Once the soap has fully melted, add the red poppy seeds and 25 drops of fragrance oil. Add the red colorant a few drops at a time, mixing thoroughly to incorporate the color, until your desired shade of red is achieved.

9. Pour soap into the mold. Set aside for a couple of hours.

10. Remove soap from the mold and slice it into bars. You can also slice each bar to make 3 triangle watermelon soaps.

Chapter 5: Soap Making Techniques

There are 4 common methods for making a bar of soap: cold process, hot process, melt and pour, and hand milling. The first two involve the use of lye, while the other two don't. Making liquid soap also requires lye.

Soap Making with Lye

When making soap using lye, you'll notice that all recipes instruct you to blend together the oil mixture and lye solution until they reach trace. This means that you'll have to blend until the two mixtures are completely mixed. If some oil remains separate, it will leave pockets of lye once transferred in the mold.

A mixture that's reached a light trace looks like a cake batter. A medium trace resembles pudding but can still be poured. A thick trace retains its shape and will likely need to be spooned to transfer into the mold.

Cold-Process Soap Making

Cold process is the method of making soap without applying any external heat to "cook" the soap. It's the most common technique used in making soap with lye.

Pros:

- You can customize every ingredient according to your preference.

- You can include fresh ingredients, such as milk and purees in the soap you're making because you have control over the saponification process.

173

- You can manipulate the trace of soap batter and be more creative by making swirls, frosting, and other effects.

Cons:

- Cold process soaps require at least 4 weeks to cure.

- It has a finicky temperature requirement. You need to make sure that the temperatures of the oils and lye solution are within 10° of each other before mixing.

- Some FD&C and mica colorants tend to morph due to the high pH environment.

How to Make Cold-Process Soap

1. Choose a recipe and assemble the required ingredients and safety gear. Prepare your mold.

2. Using a digital scale, weigh out the required amount of ingredients separately. Wear goggles and rubber gloves whenever you're handling lye.

3. In a well-ventilated area, slowly add lye to the water. Using a rubber spatula or a heavy-duty plastic spoon, stir until the lye is completely dissolved. As the lye dissolves, the mixture will get quite hot so you need to take precautions when handling it. Set the mixture aside and allow to cool to 100-120° F.

4. While the lye mixture is cooling, combine the oils in a stainless steel pot and warm them together until they're melted. You can also choose to melt the solids first before adding the liquid oils. Remove the oils from heat and allow to cool to 100-120° F.

5. To test the temperature, you can use an infrared thermometer every 5 to 10 minutes or place a candy thermometer in each container. If the lye solution is cooling faster, you can slow down the cooling process by placing the container in a warm water bath. If the oils are cooling faster, heat them up a bit.

Although mixtures are usually combined when they're between 100-120°F, you can mix them at the temperature of your choice. What's important is that the two mixtures are at 10° of each other.

6. Once both mixtures reach the desired temperatures, slowly add the lye solution to the oils. Using a stick blender, stir the mixture manually for about 30 seconds then turn the blender on and blend for another 30 seconds. Alternate until the desired consistency is achieved.

   Make sure that the blade is completely submerged before turning the blender on or you'll splash the mixture everywhere. If you're adding extras such as essential oil and colorants, bring the mixture to a light trace. If not, bring it to a medium trace.

7. Add the extras and pulse the stick blender a few times to bring the batter to a medium trace.

8. With your rubber gloves still on, quickly transfer the batter into the mold. If needed, smooth the top with a wooden spoon or rubber spatula.

   At this point, the soap is still caustic and can irritate your skin. If your skin touches the raw soap batter, rinse with cold water.

9. Insulate or freeze your soap for at least 24 hours. To insulate, cover the mold with a piece of cardboard and wrap it with a towel. If you don't want to insulate your soap, you can just leave it in the freezer.

   If you choose to insulate, check the soap once in a while. If you see any cracks forming on top, the soap is too warm and you'll have to remove the cardboard and towel.

10. Remove the soap from the mold and slice it into bars using a knife or a wire soap cutter.

11. Put the soap bars on pieces of wax paper and leave them in a dry area for 4 to 6 weeks, turning occasionally. Keep an inch between bars to allow air to circulate.

Curing is a required step for all cold-process soaps. Without it, lye won't be fully neutralized and the soap will be too harsh to the skin.

Insulate or Freeze?

Insulating your cold process soap will keep its temperature high as it hardens in the mold. The main reason for doing this is to promote the gel phase—a stage in the saponification process where soap heats up to 180°F and looks gelatinous.

Forcing your soap into the gel phase will give it a more vibrant color and a slightly shiny appearance. It also prevents the formation of soda ash—a white, ashy film that can make soap feel crumbly. Gelled soaps are also easier to remove from the mold. If you use natural colorants, such as madder root powder and turmeric, your soap will have a dull look unless they undergo the said phase.

Gel phase isn't a requirement in cold process soap making. It's more of a personal preference, affecting only the appearance of soap and not its quality. In fact, if your recipe includes fruits, honey, milk, and alternative liquids, you should freeze your soap or leave it uncovered on the counter to harden. Forcing it to gel can cause an unpleasant smell and discoloration.

Your other option is to leave your soap at room temperature without cover. Depending on the temperature of the oil and lye when you mixed them and how warm the room is, your soap may gel or not. Sometimes it can go through a partial gel phase, making the color in the middle darker than the rest.

Working with Liquids Other Than Water

Water isn't the only liquid that you can mix with lye in cold-process soap making. Goat's milk is the most popular substitute for water because it makes the soap creamier and more moisturizing. Other alternatives are coconut milk, tea, buttermilk, and beer.

It still isn't established whether the moisturizing and healing properties of these water substitutes survive after reacting with lye.

Even if they don't provide additional benefits, using them can add a personal touch to your handmade soap.

Liquids other than water react differently to lye. Usually, they produce more caustic steam, become foul-smelling, and turn brown. The bad smell won't stay in your cured soap but the reaction can be really nasty so you have to take extra precautions when working with any of them.

1. Place your container with the liquid in the sink before adding and mixing lye. Some liquids tend to bubble over and in case that happens, the solution won't spill onto the floor or counter.

2. Make sure that your work area has great ventilation. The fumes from the solution could be heavier and more foul smelling.

3. Always chill your liquid before adding the lye. It's also a good idea if you're working with just plain distilled water.

4. If you're working with milk, it should be partially frozen before adding the lye. Dissolve lye little by little, allowing the solution to cool down before adding more lye and keeping the temperature from exceeding 100°F.

5. If you're going to use a carbonated drink, such as beer, leave it on your counter for a few days, stirring frequently to make sure it's flat.

6. If you're working with a liquid that's high in sugar or contains alcohol, use it with a small batch of soap first to see how it would react with your other ingredients. It's also important to remember never to insulate this soap.

7. Work much slower than when you're using plain water.

Hot-Process Soap Making

This method of making soap is more like a variation of the cold process. Most of the steps are the same except for the added heat. The mixture is cooked in an oven or crockpot, speeding up the saponification process.

Pros:

- You can customize every ingredient according to your preference.

- Soap takes less time to harden than cold-process soap and can be used right away.

- Clean-up is relatively easier.

Cons:

- Because you're working with a thick soap batter, swirls and layers will be difficult to make.

- The high temperature can cause the scent of some essential or fragrance oils to fade.

- Adding fresh ingredients can be difficult since they tend to sear in the cooking process.

How to Make Hot-Process Soap

1. Choose a recipe and assemble the required ingredients and equipment. Prepare your mold.

2. Using a digital scale, weigh out the required amount of ingredients separately. Wear goggles and rubber gloves whenever you're handling lye.

3. In a well-ventilated area, slowly add lye to the water and stir until lye is completely dissolved. Set the mixture aside and allow to cool for about 20 minutes to 100-120° F.

4. Place the solid oils in the crockpot that's set on "low". Once melted, you can add the liquid oils.

   If you'll be using the oven instead of the crockpot, you can do this with the stove.

5. When the oils are completely liquefied, turn the crockpot off and then slowly add the lye solution. Make sure that the oils are below 180°F when you add the lye solution to avoid any negative reaction.

6. Blend the mixture using a stick blender. Make sure that the blade is completely submerged before turning the blender on or you'll splash the mixture everywhere. Bring the mixture to a trace.

7. Set the crockpot on "low". Put the lid on to minimize the amount of water escaping from the pot. If you're using the oven, heat it to no more than 170°F. Place the soap mixture in an oven-proof container with lots of extra space and follow the same instructions.

8. Normally, you'll see bubbles rising from the edges. If lots of bubbles are forming, you can gently stir down the soap mixture. If not, you can just simply leave it to cook. While it's still cooking, scrape the crockpot's sides to reduce the amount of soap forming on the sides.

9. Depending on your recipe, the soap mixture will begin to appear like Vaseline in 30 minutes to an hour. You can check if it's done by taking a small sample and rubbing it between your fingers. The soap should feel waxy.

   A more reliable way of testing for doneness is the tongue test. Touch the soap to your tongue. If there's a "zap" then your soap isn't fully cooked yet. Continue cooking until there's no more "zap".

10. If you'll be adding colorants, mix them with a little olive oil while the soap is cooking. Because your soap will be thick by the time it's cooked, the colorants won't mix well unless you pre-disperse them.

11. Once the soap is cooked, turn the heat off. Remove the crockpot sleeve from the heating pot. If you're adding any botanical extracts orbits, mix them in. Add fragrance or essential oils only when the soap's temperature is below 180°F. If fragrance is added when the temperature is still too high, the smell may not incorporate well into the soap. Add the colorants and mix.

It's important to work fast on this step as it will be a bit difficult to mix once the soap cools. It's also a good idea to heat all the additives slightly if they're cold before adding them to the soap.

For first-timers, it's best to add only one fragrance and color. If you're using several colors or want to make layers or a swirl of color, separate out some portions of soap. Add the pre-mixed colorants to the separated portions and quickly stir with a whisk.

12. Since the soap mixture is thick, you won't be able to pour it. Instead, scoop it into the mold quickly. Tap the mold filled with soap on the counter several times to get rid of any air pockets.

13. Cover the mold and set it aside. After 24 to 48 hours, you can cut the soap into bars. They can be used immediately or you can let them cure for a few weeks to allow extra water to evaporate and make the soap harder.

Liquid Soap Making

There are a few methods of making liquid soap and the most common follow the hot-process method of creating a soap paste. What differentiates liquid soap from hot- or cold-process soap is the type of lye it requires. Instead of sodium hydroxide (NaOH), liquid soap uses potassium hydroxide (KOH).

Pros:

- If you plan on selling handmade soaps, liquid soap will be more profitable.

Cons:

180

- The process is more complicated and requires a lot of patience.

How to Make Liquid Soap

1. Choose a recipe and prepare all the required ingredients and equipment. Because making liquid soap is more difficult, beginners may want to stick to a simple tried-and-tested recipe.

2. Using a digital scale, weigh out the required amount of ingredients separately. Wear goggles and rubber gloves whenever you're handling lye.

3. Place the oils in the crockpot set on low, melting the solids first before adding the liquids. Heat up the mixture to 150-170°F.

4. While the oils are in the crockpot, add lye to the water. If you notice a crackling sound, don't worry. It's normal for potassium hydroxide to react this way as it dissolves. Mix the solution completely and until it's clear.

5. When the oils are completely liquefied, slowly add the lye-water. There's no need to wait for the solution to cool first. With the stick blender still turned off, stir the lye solution and oils together.

6. Blend the mixture with the stick blender. Make sure that the blade is completely submerged before turning the blender on to keep the mixture from splashing everywhere. Bring the mixture to a medium trace with a pudding-like consistency. This could take up to 30 minutes, depending on the type of oils you're using.

7. Cover the pot with the lid. After 15 to 20 minutes, check to see if there are oils that separated. If there are, stir the mixture. Put the lid back. Check and stir the mixture every 30 minutes. It will take about 3 to 4 hours for the soap to cook.

In the time it takes to cook, the soap will transform and have different consistencies. After about 2 hours, it will become a solid taffy which is difficult to stir. Use a potato masher to break it up. Eventually, the mixture will start getting creamy.

8. Once the mixture has softened and become translucent, add an ounce of the soap paste to two ounces of boiling water. Stir and break up the soap until it's completely dissolved. If the liquid is a bit cloudy, the paste is ready. If it's cloudy or milky, the paste isn't cooked long enough. It's also possible that you've made some errors in measurement.

9. Observe the test mixture as it cools. If it stays clear, you can continue. Boil the required amount of water and pour it to the soap paste. Stir it a bit with the potato masher or a spoon. Switch off the heat and put on the lid.

   After about an hour, stir the soap some more. More likely, it's still gooey and chunky. Put the lid back on and leave it overnight to dissolve.

10. Once the paste has completely dissolved, you have to neutralize the soap before adding fragrance. A neutralizing solution is required as liquid soap uses about 10% more lye than bar soaps.

    Turn the crockpot on and bring the liquid soap up to 180°F. While the soap is heating up, mix the required amount of neutralizing solution in a separate container. You can use a 33% Borax solution or 20% boric acid solution to neutralize the soap. To make the Borax solution, add 3 oz. of Borax for every 6 oz. of boiling water. To make boric acid, add 2 oz. of Borax for every 8 oz. of boiling water.

    Prepare about ¾ ounces of this solution for every pound of soap (excluding the added water). Round down the amount of neutralizer as too much of it can make your soap cloudy.

    Once the soap mixture is hot enough, add half of the Neutralizer. Stir well and observe. If it doesn't become cloudy, add the remaining half.

11. When soap is already neutralized, you can add fragrance, if desired. Because fragrance oils may react with liquid soap, it's best to test it first on a small amount of your finished soap.

12. Allow the liquid soap to cool before transferring it into large containers. Place them in a cool place and allow the soap to rest for about a week. During this time, cloudiness should clear up and insoluble solids should settle.

13. Transfer your liquid soap into their final containers carefully to avoid disturbing the settled solids.

Soap Making without Lye

Is it really possible to make soap without using lye? The answers are both yes and no.

Lye is essential in soap making—without it, there'll be no soap. But you can still make soap without lye. Hand milling and melt-and-pour methods allow you to make handmade soaps using pre-made soaps, so there'll be no need for you to worry about handling lye.

Melt-and-Pour Soap Making

This method is the easiest way of making soap. You only have to melt pre-made soap and add your desired fragrance.

Pros:

- Soap doesn't require much time to make and can be used after it hardens, which usually takes only a few hours.

- With parental control, even kids as young as 4 will be able to make soap through this method.

- Soap doesn't have high pH so there's no need to worry about fragrance oils causing negative reactions.

- You can make layered soap with clean and straight layers.

Cons:

- Soap is prone to sweating (glycerin dew) due to the extra glycerin content.

- You can't add fresh ingredients because they will eventually go bad.

- Soap base can burn and if it does, it would be difficult to work with.

How to Make Melt-and-Pour Soap

1. Choose a recipe and assemble the required ingredients and equipment. Prepare your mold.

2. Measure out the required amount of melt-and-pour soap base and cut them into small chunks. Make sure that all the equipment you're using is clean. The soap will pick up any dirt, which will be difficult to remove. Place the soap base in a glass container.

   Some soap makers cover their container with Saran Wrap to keep the soap from drying out. Most soaps turn out fine even without doing this so it's up to you if you want to be on the safe side.

3. Place the glass container in the microwave and heat the soap up 30 seconds at a time. Take the container out and stir the soap. Repeat this step until soap is completely melted.

4. While the soap is in the microwave, measure out the required fragrance. If you're making your own soap recipe, the rule of thumb is to add 0.4 ounces of fragrance or essential oil for every pound of soap. You can use less or more depending on how strong or light your fragrance oil is.

5. Once the soap is completely melted, remove it from the microwave and add the fragrance oil. If you choose to add some color, make sure that the dye you're using is soap-safe and skin-safe. Stir the melted soap gently to blend the color and incorporate the fragrance completely.

   Avoid stirring too hard to prevent bubbles from forming. If there are bubbles, spray a little bit of rubbing alcohol to get rid of them.

6. Pour the soap into the prepared mold and cover it with Saran Wrap. Set it aside to cool and harden. It takes several hours for the soap to be ready at room temperature. If you place it in the fridge, (but never in the freezer) the soap will harden in about an hour.

7. Once the soap has completely hardened, it should be easy for you to remove the soap bars from the mold. If there are bars that won't pop out, run some hot water over the bottom of the mold. The bar should fall easily.

   Trim off any imperfections using a small knife, if desired. You can use your finished soap immediately since the soap base is already cured.

Hand-Milling Soap

Also known as re-batching, hand-milling is the process of giving new life to soap. This method involves the grating and melting of soap that's already been made and adding fragrances, colors, or any additives you want.

Hand-milling is a great way to reuse bits of leftover soap. It also offers a way to fix a batch of soap if you made a mistake.

Pros:

- You'll be able to use delicate ingredients that aren't compatible with the lye solution.

- Curing soap takes at most 2 weeks.

- Clean-up is super simple and easy.

Cons:

- You can't add fresh ingredients because they will eventually go bad.

- The high temperature can cause the scent of some essential or fragrance oils to fade.

- Swirls and layers are difficult to make because you're working with thick soap batter.

How to Hand Mill Soap

The steps described below are for fixing mistakes, but you could easily adapt the steps for the reprocessing of leftover soap.

1. If the soap you're going to use has been curing for a few days, grate it using a cheese grater. If it's still too soft to grate or freshly made, you can just chop it into small pieces.

2. Place the grated soap in a glass oven dish or into a crockpot. Add some liquid and stir the mixture gently. You can use plain water or milk (goat's, cow's, or coconut milk) to melt the soap. Assuming that you're using a week-old soap, add about 2 ounces of liquid for every pound of grated soap. It if doesn't look wet enough, add another ounce. Fresher or softer soap will require less water while older ones will need more to melt.

   You won't have to worry if you end up adding too much liquid. Your soap will only require more time to cure before it's ready to use.

3. If the mistake you're trying to fix is leaving out oil or not adding enough lye solution, you can add those at this time. Depending on the amount of lye solution you'll add, your soap may not need the liquid from the previous step. If it does, just add the liquid a little at a time.

4. Set your oven between 150°F and 170°F or your crockpot on low and put the lid on. If you're using the oven, make sure the dish is tightly covered.

5. After an hour, remove the lid and stir the mixture gently. It should be starting to liquefy and the edges should start to look

186

translucent. Put the lid back on. Allow it to cook for another hour.

6. After another hour, stir the mixture up again and mash out any lumps. Let it cook some more until it's completely softened, translucent, and pourable.

7. Once the mixture has achieved the consistency required, add any additives that you want to incorporate into your soap and stir it up well. If you're hand-milling unscented soap, start with about ½ ounce of fragrance per pound of soap.

8. Scoop the soap into your prepared mold. Push it down with a rubber spatula or spoon and tap the mold on your counter so the soap settles into the mold. Set it aside for at least 24 hours.

9. Pop the soap out of the mold and allow it to harden completely. The amount of time your soap needs to cure depends on how much liquid you added.

Tweaking a Soap Recipe

As a beginner in soap making, it's best to stick with the recipe. But sometimes, you may want to change the percentage of one or more of the oils or the oil itself. These general guidelines should help if you choose to do so.

1. Do you want to increase the amount of lather or the size of your soap's bubbles?

   - Increase the percentage of oils that add to bubble lather, such as coconut oil, babassu oil, and palm kernel oil.

   - Decrease the amount of free oils (super fat) since too much of these reduce lather.

   - Use lather-increasing additives, such as sugar, sodium lactate, sodium citrate, or rosin.

- Replace water with liquids that can boost lather, such as wine or beer.

2. Do you want to stabilize your soap's lather?

   - Use 5% to 10% of castor oil in your recipe.

   - Add or increase the percentage of oils and butters that contribute to lather, such as almond oil, lard, palm oil, sunflower oil, cocoa butter, or shea butter.

   - Decrease the percentage of oil that hinders or don't contribute much to lather, such as olive oil.

3. Do you want to increase conditioning in your soap recipe?

   - Substitute water with other liquids, such as milk, aloe vera juice, or yogurt.

   - Increase the super fat of total oils in your recipe.

   - Add or increase the percentage of nourishing oils, such as olive oil, sunflower oil, avocado oil, rice bran oil, or apricot kernel oil.

   - Use 5% to 10% of luxury oils, such as argan oil, flaxseed oil, jojoba oil, or hemp seed oil.

4. Do you want to increase the hardness of your soap?

   - Increase the percentage of hard oils or oils that are solid/semi-solid at room temperatures, such as coconut oil, babassu oil, palm oil, or lard.

   - Use 0.5% to 1% (based on total soap recipe) of stearic acid.

   - Use 1% to 5% of beeswax.

- Add 0.5 oz. of sodium lactate for every pound of oil in your recipe.

If you decide to make some changes in the recipe (even minute ones) use a lye calculator to come up with the right amount of lye. Different types of oil need different amounts of lye to turn into soap. Not using the right amount of lye can make your soap either too soft or too harsh.

Using a Lye Calculator

There are several free online lye calculators you can use if you have to make some changes in the soap recipe. The most common of which is SoapCalc.

Don't be intimidated with all the empty boxes and the values that you have to enter. Using a lye calculator isn't as hard as it looks.

1. Select the **Type of Lye** that you'll be using. The default is **NaOH**, which as you already know is the lye for making bar soaps.

2. Select the unit of measure (Pounds, Ounces, or Grams) for the **Weight of Oils** in your recipe. Enter the total weight of oils in your recipe in the box below. Remember that this weight excludes essential oils and fragrance oils.

3. **Water** refers to the amount of water that you'll be using. The default is **Water as % of oils** with a value of **38**. As a beginner, it's best to stick with this option since this is what's recommended for those who are just starting out. Decreasing the percentage of water in your recipe will make your soap reach trace faster.

4. **Super Fat** refers to the percentage of oils that won't be transformed into soap but will remain in the soap. The default value is 5%, which is the common practice in soap making. Superfatting at 5% makes soap feel more luxurious and moisturizing without inhibiting lather or making it too soft.

   You can definitely super fat your soap at a higher percentage – some soap makers even go up to 15%. However, soaps with more oils are prone to have dreaded orange spots (DOS), which are usually caused by oils that have gone rancid.

5. You don't have to make any changes under **Soap qualities and fatty acids** since this is for more experienced soap makers who want to create their own recipe. What you need to do is select the oils you'll be using from **Oils, Fats, and Waxes.**

6. Each time you select an oil, press the **Add** button under **Recipe Oil List**. If you make a mistake and have to remove oil from the list, press the **Remove** button. You can also add and remove an item by pressing "+" and "-" buttons.

   The two rightmost columns allow you to choose how you want to express the amount of oil in your recipe—either by percentage or the actual weight. Whichever you choose, enter the amount of oil you'll be using.

7. When you're done listing all the oils, press the **Calculate Recipe** button. The **Totals** row will be automatically filled. The values

should be equal to 100 and the amount you entered under **Weight of Oils.**

Click the **View or Print Recipe** button. This will display a table showing the amounts of water and lye that you should use.

Final Words

I'd like to congratulate you for transiting my lines from start to finish.

The next step is to try more advanced recipes so you can improve your skills and learn how to create more complicated designs and patterns. If you're interested, you should also discover more about the properties of soap-making oils to know how you can create your own soap recipe.

Lastly, I want to ask for a favor.

If you found any of the information that I provided in this book useful, please leave a 5-star review on Amazon.com. It's very hard to know these days which books are trustworthy and which books are there just to make a profit, and I need your help to make this book more visible and recognized.

I wish you the best of luck!

Printed in Great Britain
by Amazon